Dr. C.T.William

Dr.C.T.William

Born in Jullundur, Punjab on 21st June 1959
Father: Thomas. Mother: Rosy
Graduated in English Literature
Post Graduated in Management Studies
Master of Philosophy in Strategic Human Resource Management
Doctor of Philosophy in Human Resource Management
Researcher and Trainer in Human Resource Development
Correspondent: *Youth-N-Fashion* (English Magazine)
Printer and Publisher: *Sarovaram* (Malayalam Magazine)
Director of Documentary Films
Member: Amnesty International

Books:

Manava Vibhava VikasanaThathwachinthayum Arthashastravum (Malayalam: Philosophy, 2005)
Ithuvare (Malayalam: Poems, 2009)
Shabdham Ayodhya Vare Ethumbol (Malayalam: Criticism, 2011)
Vilapatthinte Ilakal (Malayalam: Poems, 2013)
Nakshathrangal Chuvakkunnilla (Malayalam: Travelogue, 2013)
Shesham Sheshan (Malayalam: Biography, 2013)

Address:

Dr.C.T.William
Dharmartham
Post Nettissery, Mukkattukara
Thrissur, Kerala-680 657, India
Phone: 91 9447037082
Email:
ctwilliamkerala@gmail.com
ctwilliam@hotmail.co.uk
dharmartham@gmail.com
Web: www.williamct.blogspot.com
Facebook, Twitter: Dr. C.T. William

KAUTILYA

PRAGMATIC MANAGEMENT

UNLEASHED

The Philosophy Of

Human Resource Development

and

arthashastra

Dr. C.T.William

PARTRIDGE
A Penguin Random House Company

To order additional copies of this book, contact
Partridge India
000 800 10062 62
orders.india@partridgepublishing.com

www.partridgepublishing.com/india

Dedicated to
The great soul of
My father
The great warrior of
The Indian Army

PREFACE

My acquaintance with Kautilya and the Arthashastra was limited to one-word answers to the simple questions that earned me a mark each during my school days. Later, these Mauryan reminiscences scored me more through several competitive examinations; after which, these epoch-making events faded beyond the boundaries of my boyish consciousness.

After my school days I opted for mathematics expecting that it would ensure me a more comfortable material life, instead of science in which I had performed well. Unfortunately my option turned out to be a bad investment without any return of investment.

In response to this badly invested mathematics, I experienced the socio-economic awareness of why some people become rich and other poor. This awareness switched me over to humanities specifically English literature in my degree course, being interested in creative writing. However, I soon realized that studying literature and scribbling literature are two quite different exercises.

Then there was a decade-long unproductive silence and non-violence. During which I detached myself from all physical and meta-physical attachments. Anarchy ruled my spirit and conscience. I had struggled to explore more of myself.

Time broke the passive silence and I entered government service. My encounter there with the bureaucratic barons changed my psyche. A spirit of academic unrest and frustration sparked my inner conscience. The spark gave me a fresh focus and fascination to the powerful strategic management which is oriental in spirit rather than occidental in muscle.

Discontented with the present iterating administrative environment and disillusioned with the bad spirit of socio-political unrest, I was led to the glorious age-old pastures of India-the golden age of Mauryan Empire. There I found a wonderful flame. My eyeballs focused for a sharp vision. To my surprise, the flame flooded with oriental spiritual brilliance. Kautilya, the luminous sphere was appeared. I was astounded to discover the historic brilliant treasures earned by the great Kautilya.

I was recapturing my lost decade. A new productive decade dawned. I have rediscovered and reinvented the great Kautilya-the tantric guru of the Mauryan Empire. Kautilya, the precursor of modern management strategies was thus resurrected. The invincible savior of global administration emerged.

The Mauryan warship that could not be anchored was at last anchored. The Mauryan warhorse that could not be leashed was at last leashed. The unquenchable spirit of the great Kautilya is now unleashed. Enjoy its spiritual dimensions, knowledge and radiance.

Dr. C.T. William

FOREWORD

Kautilya Unleashed' is a courageous and innovative attempt by Dr. C.T.William to analyze the management principles behind the successful working of the Mauryan Empire, India's first great empire in archeologically recorded history to rule most of the Indian subcontinent. The trail of the search inevitably leads to Kautilya, who served as the chief advisor to the founder of the empire Chandragupta and later his son Bindusara, and to his seminal treatise "Arthashastra" (Economics), which is widely perceived as the precursor to the classical economics of the post-industrial world almost 20 centuries later and its branches such as management science.

In the modern world, Human Resources Development (HRD) has increasingly being identified as one of the key factors which determines the levels and pace of the growth of organizations. In fact, HRD is now an integral part of the science of organizational management and it has been defined as the framework for the expansion of human capital within an organization through the development of both the organization and the individual to achieve performance improvement.

Dr. William has identified two key elements in "Arthashastra" which corresponds to the above principles. The first is that of the principle of 'Acquisition of Resources' which he links with the HRD process by which employees of an organization are assisted in a continuous and planned way to acquire and sharpen capabilities to perform various functions associated with their present or expected future roles, develop their general capabilities as individuals and discover and exploit their potential for their own or organizational development purposes. The second is the principle of 'Retention of Acquired Resources' which implies the development of an organizational culture in which superior-subordinate relations, teamwork and collaboration are strong factors which contributes to the professional well-being, motivation and pride of the employees.

The current trend towards an increasingly globalized environment has led to the desire to learn and understand the dynamics and historical and sociological roots of various cultures and models of social and business organization other than that of one's own. The recent proliferation of studies analyses and books on Sun Tzu's "The Art of War" and Machiavelli's "The Prince" are a pointer to this phenomenon. In that context, a study, such as the one attempted here by Dr. William on Kautilya and Arthashastra, is most timely. I am sure that this work will serve as a path breaker for more such studies in the field of modern business management, not only in India but across the world, on India's proven successes in producing effective systems of social administration and human management in ancient times.

Dr. Shashi Tharoor

CONTENTS

KAUTILYA

PRAGMATIC MANAGEMENT
UNLEASHED

AUTHOR'S NOTE

Alphabetic abbreviations Ab, Cd....: Indicate Book, Chapter, Verse. Arthashastra consists of 15 Books 150 Chapters and 195 Subjects discussed. Since the number of verses varies from translation to translation, exact number could not be recorded. For example, {Bk.1.Ch.1.Vs.1}-Book 1, Chapter 1, Verse 1. Mbh- Indicates Mahabharata.

Arabic Numerals 1, 2, 3 ... Indicate the number of the verse. For example, {Bk.1.Ch.1.Vs.1}-Book Number 1, Chapter Number 1, Verse Number 1. Verse Numbers are as in the translation of R.P. Kangle, The Kautilya Arthashastra, Part I (Text) and Part II (Translation), Second edition; University of Bombay 1969.

Double Brackets {}: Enclose full reference of the verse. For example, {Bk.1.Ch.1.Vs.1}-Book Number 1, Chapter Number 1, Verse Number 1.

Squire Brackets [ ]: Enclose translator's interpretations and comments. For example, This epigram can be equated with the Marxian philosophy where in the final stage "the state withers away" and the people are ruled automatically even without a ruler [*Nayak*]. In Marxian philosophy, the concept of human asset or capital is treated as the proletariat; the community of the working class. It is this proletariat that in its final stage attains socialism [*Yogakshema*] and the state withers away. In Kautilyan context, this is a process of automation with *Prithvilabham* (The acquisition of *Yogakshema* [socialist state] and *Prithvipalanam* (The retention of the *Yogakshema* [socialist state].

Sanskrit and Malayalam words: Presented in italics; diacritical marks are not used. For example, Kautilya's Arthashastra showered and still showering the oriental brilliance of Human Resource Management and development through the philosophy of *Prithvilabham* (Acquisition) and *Prithvipalanam* (Retention). Some Malayalam words are taken from the translation by K.V.M. *Kautilyante* Arthashastra, Kerala Sahithya Academy, Thrissur, 1998.

Courtesy: *Kautilya-The Arthashastra* by L.N. Rangarajan, Penguin Books India 1992.

Dr. C.T. William

"Kautilya's Arthashastra
showered and still showering the oriental brilliance of Human Resource Management and development through the
ever-acclaimed philosophy of *Prithvilabham* (Acquisition) and
Prithvipalanam (Retention)."

chapter-1

INTRODUCTION

H RD, the three lettered abbreviation of Human Resource Development has become a widely applicable Human Resource Management concept all around the world. At the same time this trend-setting Human Resource Management concept is under the applicability test in the laboratories of the modern management and political gurus. The question is regarding the micro as well as the macro dimensions of its application in the Organizational - Corporate level and the State - National level.

In the midst of these experiments and commotions evolved, many personal managers and their organizations have made HRD a synonym for their training and development department. A major segment of organizations around the globe has christened their personal department as HRD department.

It was Leonard Naddler who in 1969 formally introduced the concept of HRD while presenting a paper in a conference organized by the American Society for Training and Development (www.astd.com). Naddler has defined HRD as "those learning experiences which are organized for a specific time and designed to bring about the possibility of behavioral change." Here the 'organized learning experiences' implies the *acquisition* of resources and 'bringing about the possibility of behavioral change' implies the *retention* of the acquired resources. We shall see how this echoes Kautilyan concept of Human Resource Development.

The noted Indian HRD Guru T. Venkateswara Rao (1986) who extensively worked on the subject has further defined HRD as a process by which employees of the organization are helped in a continuous and planned way to: acquire and sharpen capabilities to perform various functions associated with their present or expected future roles [*Acquisition* of resources]; develop their general capabilities as individuals and discover and exploit their potentials for their own or organizational development purposes [*HRD*];and to develop an organizational culture in which superior-subordinate relationship, teamwork and collaboration among sub-units are strong and contribute to the professional well-being, motivation and pride of employees [*Retention* of the acquired resources].

These enabling factors motivate the management areas including organization structures, organization climate, HRD climate, HRD knowledge and skills of managers, HR planning, recruitment and selection, performance and potential appraisal, career planning and development, training, management development, organizational development, social and cultural programs, worker's participation management (WPM) and quality circles (QC) and other HRD functions. As we noted earlier, these areas are generally focused *to acquire* the resources for the growth of the organization and *to retain* the resources for the making of good individuals, dynamic groups and society.

1.1. Mechanical Resources Vs. Human Resources.

With the emergence of Globalization and Information technology, Robots and Computers have redefined or restructured the above-mentioned human resource factors. Consequently, people have declined into a mere machinery to work for the organization's productivity. Thus the value-embedded society has terribly lost the value-added productive concept of Human Capital. This has miss-fired the theory of acquisition of resources and retention of the acquired resources.

Chandragupta Maurya

The spirit of Globalization and the sprint of Information technology have substantially crippled the biological, intellectual and emotional growth and development of human resources of every nation in the world. The world has been impoverished into a museum of programmable human beings. Nations are competing with each other and struggling for their own individual existence and national prosperity. This forward movement has thus become tougher and they have started a backward movement to explore the valuable treasures of the past for additional rejuvenation to ensure the future prospects and existence of the humanity.

1.2. Kautilya Arthashastra and Human Resource

The phenomenal negation of Human Capital in our time has forced us on a backward journey to the golden history of the ancient India during the golden period of Chandragupta Maurya (321 BC-298 BC), where Kautilya's Arthashastra showered and is still showering the oriental brilliance of Human Resource Management and Development through the ever-acclaimed philosophy of *Prithvilabham* (Acquisition) and *Prithvipalanam* (Retention).

Kautilya

The aim of this book is to explore the oriental Human Resource Management and Human Resource Development strategies as designed by the great Kautilya and to re-apply them in the present micro and macro dimensions of Organizations or Nations.

My book also traces a journey back to the royal labyrinths of Arthashastra of Kautilya, bed -rocked on the philosophy of *Prithvilabham* (Acquisition of resources) and *Prithvipalanam* (Retention of the acquired resources) .This golden philosophy had once guided the nation to healthy co-existence and prosperity. Apart from the discussions on the human resource management and development, an attempt is also being made to depict and adapt the politics, economy, judiciary and social security system which prevailed during the period of Arthashastra to give the reader a complete pragmatic experience of the world of Arthashastra and bring it into the context of modern administrative system.

" The salary scale shall be such as to enable the accomplishment of state activities (by attracting the Right type of people), shall be adequate for meeting the bodily needs of the state servants and shall not be in contradiction to the principles of *Dharma* and *Artha*."

chapter-2

KAUTILYA EXPLORED

The Philosophy of Human Resource Development (HRD) and the science of economic liberalization have ideologically synthesized later. Dr. P. Subba Rao (1996) has described this synthesis as follows: - "HRD assumes significance in view of the fast changing organizational environments and the need of the organization to adopt new techniques in order to respond to these environmental changes. The changing environmental factors include unprecedented increase in competition within and outside the country consequent upon the announcement and implementation of economic liberalizations." It is this reinvented Strategy of Human Resource Development (HRD) that enables the society to overcome such unprecedented increase in competitive trends. It is this scientific Human Resource Planning (HRP) that capacitates the society for these tasks and the capacity will certainly work in the present as well as in the future.

In the modern context, where the role of HRD has been considered as decisive in the process of enhancing the efficiency of Administration and Management; the pragmatic administrative solutions as envisaged in Arthashastra are remarkably relevant. Kautilya recommended a judicious mix of monitoring, inspection and implementation of good wages among human resource. He understood the needs, nature and aspirations of workers. For example, he (Subramanian, 2000, p. 108) stated "One should avoid the country where there is no reward for work, no activity, no relatives or no means of learning." According to Kautilya [p. 283] "The king shall have the work of Heads of Departments inspected daily, for men are, by nature, fickle and, like horses, change after being put to work [Bk.2.Ch.9.Vs.2,4.}. " It was impossible for the king to supervise the Heads of Departments personally because they were stationed at distant locations. Therefore, the king should pay incentive wages to the Heads of Departments and also get their work inspected to reduce shirking. Similarly, he prescribed [p. 289] that the Administrator or Chancellor and the Treasurer would be paid 24000 *Panas* annually, "enough to make them efficient in their work." Such a high reward should be compared to the yearly minimum wage for an unskilled worker, which was only 60 *Panas* at this time. These facts prove that those modern practical administrative solutions have the nature of a successful continuum from the past to present.

The Philosophy of Human Resource Development (HRD) that is widely discussed among the Gurus of the modern administration and management, still exploring the unfathomable possibilities of human resource management in their management school laboratories. Hence, the ultimate aim of my book is always the pragmatic application of HRD in the areas of administration and management of the simple organization to the complex people management of the state administration.

It is believed that Leonard Naddler was the first management thinker who drafted the concept of Human Resource Development (HRD). He had introduced the concept through the research paper he presented in the American Society for Training and Development during 1969. He has defined Human Resource Development (HRD) as "those learning experiences which are organized, for a specific time, and designed to bring about the possibility of behavioral change". This definition of Naddler is but a blank statement of an earlier interpreter of the colonial administration. Later this blank statement on management thought along with its after effects has been imposed on the global management community.

The concept of Human Resource Development (HRD) formulated by Naddler, has confronted many transitions later and finally entered the arena of innovative educational methods, sociological developments and observations of behavioral science. Spengler [1971, p. 74] summarizes Kautilya's human resource management policies as follows: "His analysis, of course, was implicit, not explicit; it rested upon the assumption that individual behavior could be controlled in large measure through economic rewards and penalties, particularly when these were commensurate with the action to be encouraged or discouraged. Accordingly, while Kautilya looked at economic issues through the eyes of an economic administrator, he was aware that rules must fit man's economic propensities and foster rather than repress useful economic activity."

Kautilya understood the importance of virtue ethics and believed that they were sources of 'joy and bliss'. He confined his discussion primarily to action-oriented ethical principles and vigorously advanced them as essential to the maintenance of law and order, and to the promotion of economic development. According to Kautilya, a king must set high ethical standards, be a person displaying the highest moral character and must ensure that his successor was equally 'noble'.

The Greek philosophers Plato and Aristotle also considered ethical values as virtues, emphasized the building of a person's good character and believed that good conduct would naturally follow. (Post et al [2002, p. 129) notes: "Moral values acknowledged by Aristotle include courage, temperance, justice, and prudence. St. Thomas Aquinas added the Christian values of faith, hope, and charity to the list of morally desirable virtues. Additional virtues include honesty, compassion, generosity, fidelity, integrity, and self-control."

Plato

While Aristotle addressed the principle of virtue ethics he did not discuss any action-oriented principles of ethics. Kautilya referred to both virtue ethics and action-oriented principles of ethics. But he elaborated only on the action-oriented ethical values, such as, the golden rule, rights, fairness, and servant leadership. He (Subramanian, p. 83) wrote: "Proper behavior is more important than being virtuous." Kautilya was well educated in Vedas and philosophy but he thought that a discussion regarding personal character-building was beyond the scope of the Arthashastra. For example, he stated [p. 142] a prince "Should learn philosophy and the three Vedas from authoritative teachers, economics from the heads of [various government] departments, and the science of government from [not only] theoretical exponents of political science [but also] from practicing politicians."

Aristotle

2.1. Empowering Factors of HRD.

The three enabling factors that bring Human Resource Development (HRD) to the forefront of Human Resource Management are that they help to: -

1) Acquire or sharpen capabilities required to perform various functions associated with their present or expected future roles.[*Acquisition* of resources]

2) Develop their general capabilities as individuals and discover and exploit their own inner potentials for their own or organizational purposes.[*HRD*]

3) Develop organizational culture in which superior-subordinate relationship, team work and collaboration among subunits are strong and contribute to the professional well-being, motivation and pride of employees.[*Retention* of the acquired resources]

2.2. Kautilya and conceptual analysis of HRD.

The great Kautilya and his conceptual analysis of HRD are to be discussed in this context; because Kautilya has worked out his concept of Human Resource Development (HRD) based on the Indian culture bed-rocked by *Dharma, Artha, Kama* and *Moksha* [*Purushartha*]. All human resource activities including the salary administration are to be placed before the principles of *Purushartha*. " The salary scale shall be such as to enable the accomplishment of state activities (by attracting the Right type of people), shall be adequate for meeting the bodily needs of the state servants and shall not be in contradiction to the principles of *Dharma* and *Artha*" {Bk.5.Ch.3.Vs. 2.}. Here the salary scale is commensurate with the accomplishment of the state-building activities and the maintenance of individual existential needs; both adhering to the principles of *Dharma, Artha, Kama* and *Moksha* [*Purushartha*]. There was in fact a strict maintenance and control of this principle and its phases of implementation; which often alleged as monarchical imposition on people. This monarchical imposition has invited sharp criticism from the Marxist schools of thinkers and ideologists. But this monarchical interference is not an attack on the fundamental freedom of the individual or the society as alleged, but a powerful patriotic process of acquisition of the human asset or capital [*Prithvilabham*] and the pragmatic process of retention of the acquired skills and knowledge [*Prithvipalanam*].

"In the interests of the prosperity of the country, a King
should be diligent in foreseeing the possibility of calamities,
try to avert them before they arise, overcome those which
happen, remove all obstructions to economic activity
and prevent loss of revenue to the state."

chapter-3

KAUTILYA AND INDIAN VISION

Kautilya was the first pragmatic diplomat and an exceptional intellectual giant who has invested strenuous intellectual effort in the areas of Philosophy, Political diplomacy, Political science, Political economics, Law, Human Resource Management and Development, Political Administration, Physics, Metaphysics, Psychology, Logic and other Moral sciences. The Return Of Investment (ROI) has been optimized by his tremendous research outputs. He has codified all written and unwritten forms of historical and pre-historical records and edited those scattered fragments of royal sciences and knowledge, unearthed from the past history of ancient India. The codified and edited records are then analyzed and the analytical findings were skillfully woven to form the well-known book Arthashastra; the kaleidoscope that reflects the multi-dimensional cause and effect phenomenon of the human being, society, rites, rituals, culture, philosophy, administration, laws, politics and economics of the ancient India.

History claims that Kautilya, the father of political administration and the author of Arthashastra was the first pragmatic political diplomat who transformed Chandragupta, the founder of Maurya dynasty into the great emperor of *Aryavartha*. Ancient Indian history marks the age of Chandragupta as the indelible and eventful golden age of political administration and political economics. No doubt, the cerebral chip behind this historic golden age is the phenomenal management processor and the first oriental management guru, Kautilya.

Chandraguptam nrupam rajye Kautilya sthapavishyathi
Chathurvimsal sama rajye chandragupto bhavishyathi

The couplet cited above from *Vayu Purana* supports the historical fact that Kautilya lived during the age of Chandragupta Maurya and he was the master-mind behind the dynamic animation of the Great Chandragupta Maurya. Supporting the fact, Dr. R. Shamashastry, the great explorer of Arthashastra and the translator of the English version (*Kautilya's Arthashastra, The Indian Antiquary, A Journal Of Oriental Research, Vol. XXXIV, 1905)* quotes a prediction from the *Vishnu Purana* 4th canto, 24th chapter, regarding the fantastic appearance of Kautilya. This prediction, incidentally, was scribed fifty centuries ago, nearly 2700 years be-

Dr R Shamashastry

fore this political heavyweight and man of destiny was to appear. The prediction informs us: "(First) *Mahapadma* then his sons - only nine in number - will be the lords of the earth for a hundred years. A *Brahmin* named Kautilya will slay these *Nandas*. On their death, the Mauryas will enjoy the earth. Kautilya himself will install Chandragupta on the throne. His son will be *Bindusara* and his son will be *Ashokavardhana.*" Thus he became the most respected king-maker, the world ever has seen. Similar prophecies are also repeated in the *Bhagavata*, *VayuPurana* and *Matsya Purana.*

Research scholars have thus explored the precious archives of the time and found that Kautilya was also known as *Vishnugupta, Chanakya, Dhramila and Angula.* The *slokas* from *Thrikandasesham* of *Purushothama Devan* supports this multi-nomenclature of Kautilya.

> *Vishnuguptasthu kautilyaschanakyo dhramilangula:*
> *Thrikandasesham*

Purushothama Devan

However the scholars have derived an inference that the name 'Kautilya' is the most acceptable one as he belongs to the *Gothra* of *Kutala* and son of *Hrishi Chanaka* lived in the *Chanaka dhesa.*

3.1. Composition and Authoring of Arthashastra.

There is a lot of disagreement and puzzlement among the scholars about the date of composition of Arthashastra and the exact period of Kautilya. This is due to the collisions and interpolations of data about the society and the customs and manners followed by the people in Arthashastra. This society is seen to have been influenced by the culture of Pre-Buddhism and experienced the continuum of the culture of the later period of *Manusmriti*. L.N. Rangarajan quotes, "though Kautilya wrote long after the time of Buddha, who died in 486 B.C., the state of society portrayed in the Arthashastra is, in the main, Pre-Buddhistic. On the other hand, the norms under which Hindu society has functioned for the last two millennia are those of *Smritis*; the earliest and most important of these, the *Manusmriti* was codified sometime in the first two centuries A.D......In fact, it is the comparison of the data in the Arthashastra with that in other works and the question of who borrowed from whom that prompts scholars to ascribe different dates to the Arthashastra itself". At the same time we have also some authentic reference to Arthashastra from the well-known *Dasakumaracharitham* written by *Dhandi* in AD 700.

> *Adheeswa thavaDhandaneetham:*
>
> *Iyamidhaneemacharya vishnuguptenu*
>
> *Mauryartha shadbee*
>
> *Sloka sahasraia samshiptha*

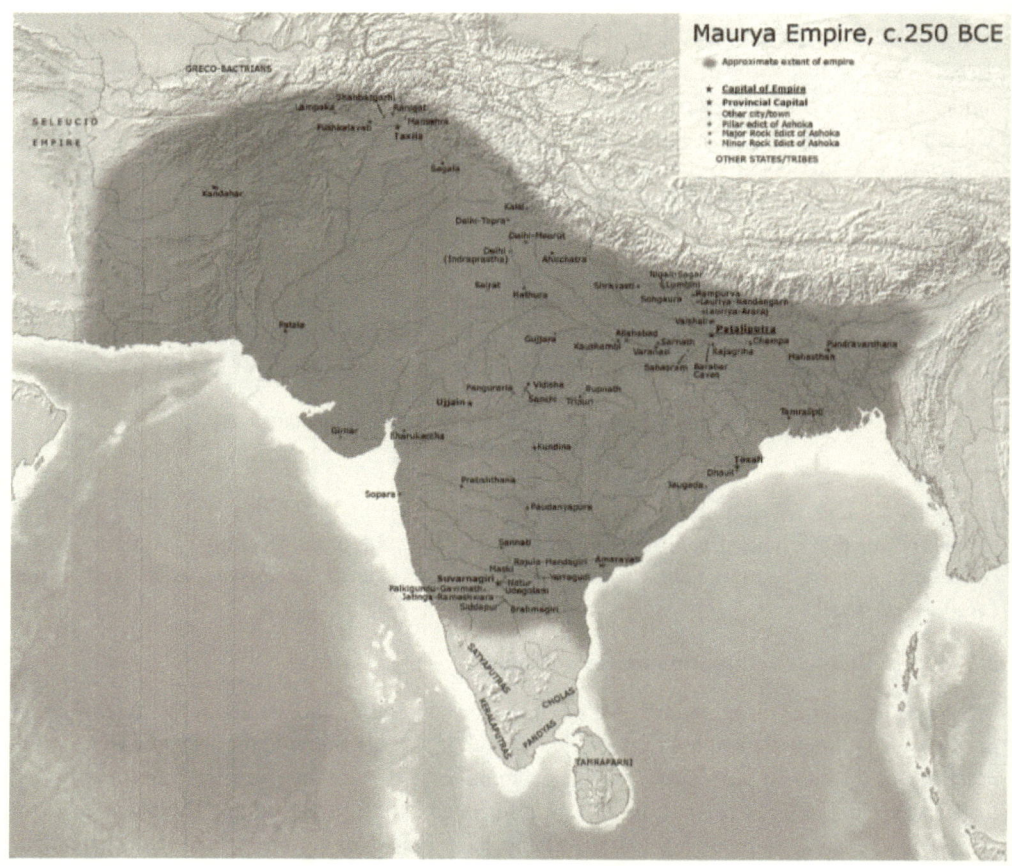

The Mauryan Empire-250 BCE

It is translated that 'the science of Politics and Economics was abridged by *Vishnugupta-charya* (Kautilya) in six thousand *Granthas* (*Sutras*) for the guidance of the Mauryans, in the hope that a well-digested study of, and administration according to the precepts of the Ar-thashastra will enable the king to conduct his rule with brilliant success'. *(Dr. R. Shamashastry, Kautilya's Arthashastra, The Indian Antiquary, A Journal Of Oriental Research, Vol. XXXIV, 1905)*. Besides, the book, Arthashastra itself tells us its origin thus:- " This *Shastra*," says the author at the end of the book, "has been written by him who, with knowledge in his head and weapon in his hand, snatched with irresistible force, the earth from Nanda." After a long debate it has been probabilistically marked the period of the Arthashastra has been marked as probably somewhere between BC 321 – BC 298; assuming that Kautilya lived during this period and served Chandragupta Maurya as his able minister and advisor. *Fig: 1.* Amidst these chronological puzzlements, the scholars of ancient Indian history have converged their research unanimously to the fact that Kautilya was an authentic interpreter of social traditions, ethnic equations, management concepts and the economic and political aspirations of his epoch.

Arthashastra, the Bible of political administration and diplomacy, combines to form a blend of curious speculations on physics, psychology, logic, ethics, metaphysics and political administration. I.N. Menon states, "Arthashastra is a sustained effort at treating in an exhaustive if not thoroughly systematic manner a variety of social, economic and political and management problem in the light of antecedent historical evolution and contemporary political and inter-state organization". {Foreword by I.N. Menon, *Kautilya Arthashastra* by K.V.M., 1935.}

Arthashastra is considered to be the first incomparable doctoral thesis written on political diplomacy. The book itself has shown the fact that Kautilya has conducted a series of in-depth studies and research analysis about the subject. This analytical quality of Kautilya is very much evident while citing his own views in contrast with those of other scholars on the controversial points of economics and political administration; the author always uses such phrases as: - "But Kautilya says thus," or "Kautilya objects to it," implying that Kautilya has applied his analytical skill to test the hypothesis. Accordingly many errors which crept into the pre-versions of Arthashastra have been traced out and removed and an attempt has been made to pronounce a final judgment with precise words, doctrines and sense on Arthashastra. "This Arthashastra is a compendium of almost similar treatises, composed by ancient teachers, on the acquisition and protection of territory. Easy to grasp and understand, free from verbosity, Kautilya has composed this treatise with precise words, doctrines and sense" {Bk.1.Ch.1.Vs.1, 19.}.

3.2. Prince of Machiavelli and Arthashastra of Kautilya.

This treatise on government is often compared to that of *The Prince* of Machiavelli. Based on this comparison, some scholars have attempted to call Kautilya as the Indian Machiavelli. But this attempt is simply an outcome of superfluous observations. Machiavelli's treatise on government was rejected with horror by almost all early readers. It was an accurate description of the means by which rulers are helped to remain and cling to power. Whereas in Arthashastra; the rulers are helped to win the hearts of the people and the state through the accurate exercise of providing welfare and prosperity to the people. According to Kautilya, ruler's duties towards the internal administration of the country are three-fold:_Rakshana_ or protection of the state from external aggression, *Palana* or maintenance of law and order within the state, and *Yogakshema* or safeguarding the welfare of the state These three basic constituents also implies strong patriotism and nationalism. Paul Brians has remarked that "although often compared to Machiavelli's *The Prince* because of its sometimes ruthless approach to practical politics.

Kautilya's work is far more varied and entertaining than usual accounts of it indicate. He mixes the harsh pragmatism for which he is famed with compassion for the poor, for slaves, and for women. He reveals the imagination of a romancer in imagining all manner of scenarios which can hardly have been commonplace in real life". (www.wsu.edu)

3.3. *Kautilya's theory of* Prithvilabham *and* Prithvipalanam.

Arthashastra has three authentic and original editions to its credit. One edition was published in 1906 in the Indian Antiquary by the Mysore Shyamasasthrikal.The second edition was published through the Punjab Sanskrit Series written by Dr. Julius Jolly in 1926 and the third edition was from Trivandrum, written by Mahamahopadhyayan Dr. Ganapathi Sasthrikal during 1924-1925.

Niccolo Machiavelli

Arthashastra has been acclaimed as an effective panacea to energize and stabilize the state administration or any organizational administration subject to certain political and geographical limitations. The cultural composition of this panacea includes mainly the philosophy of *Prithvilabham* (Acquisition) and *Prithvipalanam* (Retention) of what is acquired. According to Kautilya, *Prithvi* is the money (*Artha*) or any equivalent material resources such as territory or land. In the modern management point of view, *Prithvi* is the other form of people force or human resources. "The people of a society, whatever their *Varna* or stage of life, will follow their *Dharma* and pursue with devotion their occupations, if they are protected by the King and just use of *Dhanda* [coercion and punishment]" {Bk.1.Ch4.Vs.16.}. The dignity of human labour and the value of human resources are seen accounted for, when the King addresses the soldiers that he too, like others draws salary for the service done to the state. Hence he should also share the same status with them. This is exactly the essence of Human Resource Management.

Thulyavethanomsi bharath bhusha
Bojyamitham rajyam

The book, known for its practical theories of economics and administration, mainly concentrates on the making of an able King, Kingdom and a perfect patriotic welfare state. Kautilya says, "There cannot be a country without people and there is no Kingdom without a country" {Bk.13.Ch.4.Vs.5.}. Kautilya further explains, "In the interests of the prosperity of the country, a King should be diligent in foreseeing the possibility of calamities, try to avert them before they arise, overcome those which happen, remove all obstructions to economic activity and prevent loss of revenue to the state" {Bk.8.Ch.4.Vs.50, 21}. The result of these patriotic and pragmatic visions was the emergence of the Chandragupta Maurya, the King and a diligent foreseer; the "Gem of Indian history" and the welfare state; *Pataliputra. Fig: 2.*

Kautilya had his higher education from the well-known Learning Centre *Thakshasila* of ancient India. At *Thakshasila* he learnt Science, Philosophy, *Ayurveda*, Grammar of various languages, Mathematics, Econo mics, Astrology, Geography, Astronomy, Surgery, Agriculture, Archery and Ancient and Modern sciences. It was the exceptional skills that he learnt from *Thakshasila* enabled him to expel the cruel autocrat *Dhananadha*, the King of *Nandha* dynasty who has imposed drastic hardships and atrocities on the people of the country. The effective

weapon animated in human form; he sharpened and targeted for expelling *Dhananadha* was, Chandragupta Maurya. Kautilya, as per historical records, has trained Chandragupta Maurya for a period of eight years. The training was based on the strategic philosophy of Arthashastra and he was sociologically, psychologically and physically and metaphysically armed enough to charge the *Dhananadha* to uproot the whole *Nandha* dynasty.

Thakshasila

The philosophy on which Arthashastra was designed and structured was the harmonized forms of Dharma, Artha, Kama, and Moksha. These four constituents are in aggregate known as the Purushartha. It was the proportionate composition of these philosophic constituents that framed the Kautilyasutra which enabled the King to accomplish the philosophy of Prithvilabham (Acquisition) and Prithvipalanam (Retention) and ultimately resulted in the formation of a welfare state with people complying Purushartha. This is epigrammatized in the quote, "It is the people who constitute a Kingdom; like a barren cow, a Kingdom without people yields nothing" {Bk.7Ch.11.Vs.24, 25}.3.4.Kautilya: The Vivekananda of Aryavartha and his India visions.

These *Sutras* of Kautilya altogether centralize on the basic theory that **ends justify the means**. While treading through the means, Kautilya had his own Indian visions which can be summarized as follows:-

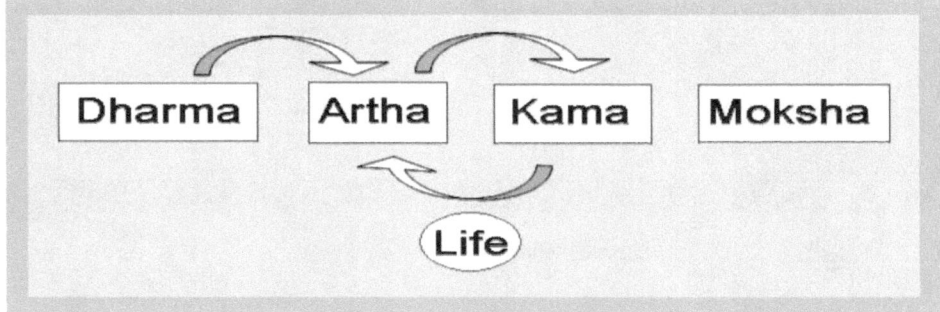

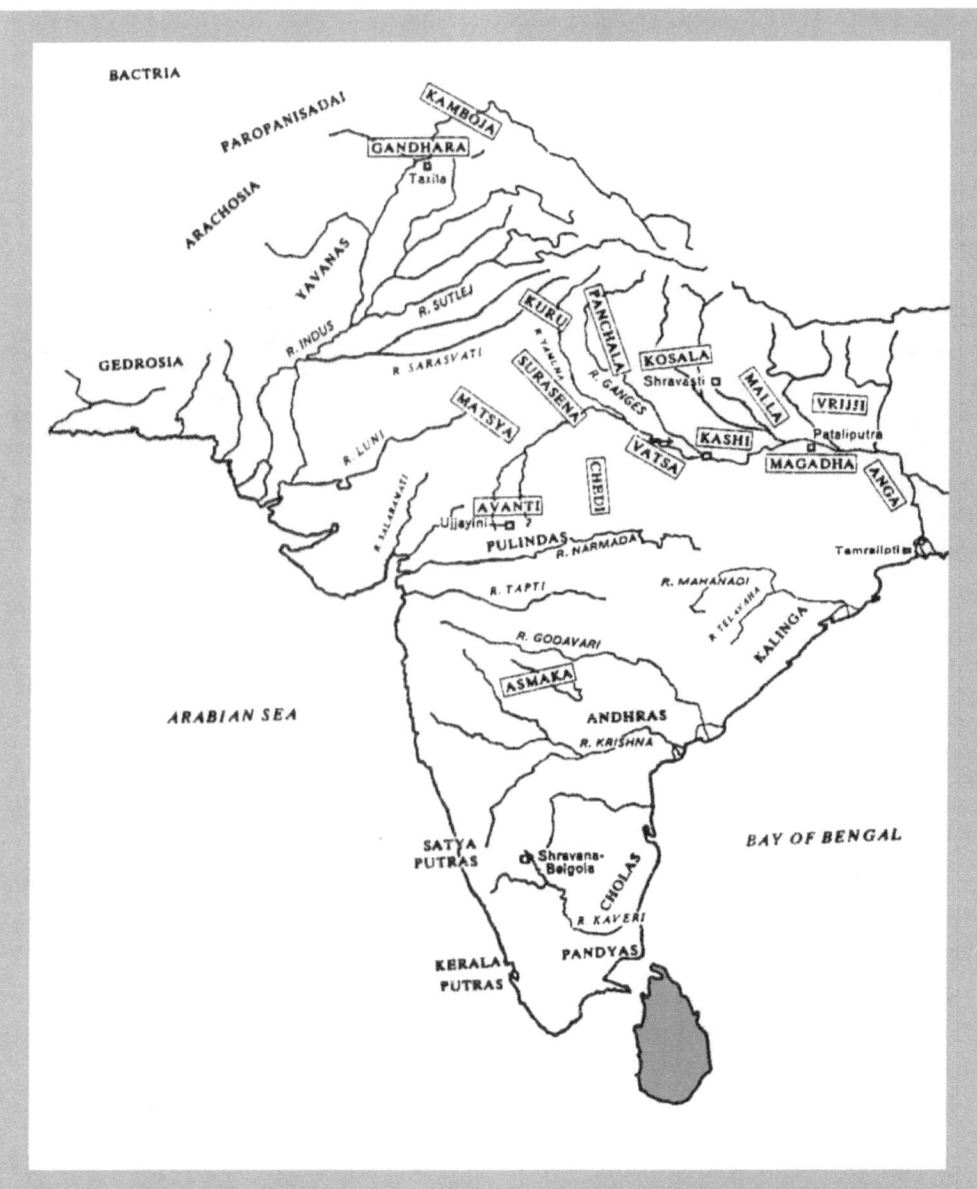

The sub continent in kautilyan times

1) A Self Sufficient Economic India that is not servile to foreign trade.

2) An egalitarian society where there are equal opportunities of prosperity for all.

3) An India which concentrates on the establishment and enrichment of new colonies for the augmentation of resources and also for the development of the already established colonies. Establishment of colonies does not mean colonization, but can be simply interpreted as the development and enrichment of natural and man-made resources.

4) An India that keeps a deep concern over the excess land and its valuable resources occupied unauthorized and underutilized by the landlords.

5) An India that takes care of the complete development process of agriculture in all seasons.

6) An India that protects the country from invasions and that provides complete social and cultural security to the people through its strategically designed forts and cities.

Swami Vivekananda

7) An India that encourages internal trade and commerce policies and stabilize the economy by way of optimum application of tax and trading.

8) An India where justice is exercised equally for all without any discrimination.

9) An India where women are protected by the state and society from social exploitation and the uncouth behaviour of men.

10) An India with spiritually balanced development.

These visions infers that like the great revolutionary and visionary *Swami Vivekananda*, Kautilya also would have stormed and shocked the whole conscience of ancient India- *Aryavartha*, 2300 years ago, with the same *mantra*:—'Arise, awake and stop not till the goal is reached' *(Uttishtatha! Jagrata! Prapya varan nibhodhata!)*.

"The source of the livelihood of men is
Artha (Wealth); that is to say, the territory
[and the inhabitants following various professions] is the wealth
[of a nation].
The science by which territory is acquired and maintained
[retained] is Arthashastra - the science of wealth and welfare"

chapter-4

ARTHASHASTRA
AND CONTENT STRUCTURE

The commandments and thoughts that fill Arthashastra have been strongly influenced by the under-currents of ancient Indian culture and philosophy. These commandments and thoughts indebted to various *Shastras* had been existed in the ancient India even before the period of Kautilya. This is highly resonant in the vibrant verses of *Mahabharatha*. There is a concrete reference to Arthashastra in *Mahabharatha* where *Arjuna* is referred to:

> *Samaptha vachane thasmi-*
>
> *nnartha Shastra visaradha-*
>
> *partho Dharmartha thathwajno*
>
> *jagou vakyamadhindritha*
>
> (Mahabharatha-Santhiparvam-161-9)

Arthashastra was structured in fifteen books which are named as *Adhikarana* {Bk.} written in the form verse or *Sutra* {Vs.}. Each *Adhikarana* consists of chapters {Ch.} and each chapters deal with different subjects under the heading *Prakarana*. Each *Prakarana* consists of different headings and sub headings. At the close of every *Adhikarana*, the summary of the *Adhikarana* is comprised in a *Sloka*. As of now researchers have discovered 15 *Adhikarana*, 180 *Prakaranas*, 150 Chapters and 195 Subjects discussed in Arthashastra.

Arthashastra has been conveniently divided into three parts I. *Thanthras*, II. *Avapam*, III. *Prakeernakas*. Of which *Thanthra* consisting of 5 *Adhikaranas* contains 106 Subjects mainly dealing with the administrative strategies to retain the resources acquired; based on the philosophy of *Prithvipalanam* (Retention), *Avapam* consists of 8 *Adhikaranas* contains 84 Subjects mainly dealing with the strategies on foreign policy; based on the philosophy of *Prithvilabham*

Mahabharata

- 31 -

(Acquisition) and *Prakeernaka* consists of 2 *Adhikarana* contains 5 Subjects dealing with the miscellaneous strategies other than *Prithvipalanam* (Retention) and *Prithvilabham* (Acquisition). The finally available and generally approved structure of Arthashastra is given in *Fig.:3*.

Figure: 3
Content Structure of the Arthashastra

Sl.No.	Name of the Adhikarana	No.of Subjects discussed
	Thanthras	
1	Vinayadhikarakam	21
2	Adhyakshapracharam	40
3	Dharmastheeyam	25
4	Kandakasodhanam	13
5	Yogavrutham	7
	Total	**106**
	Avapam	
6	Mandalayoni	2
7	Shadgunyam	32
8	Vysanadhikarikam	8
9	Abhiyasyalkarmam	12
10	Samgramikam	13
11	Sanghavrutham	2
12	Abaliyasm	9
13	Dhurgalampopayam	6
	Total	**84**
	Prakeernakas	
14	Aupanishadhikam	4
15	Thanthrayukthi	1
	Total	**5**
	Grand Total	**195**

4.1. Arthashastra and the generalized facts.

The research on the commandments and thoughts that enriched Arthashastra has brought forth the following facts:

1) It is a historical phenomenon that the control of all administrative machinery will ultimately reach the hands of a Monarch during its evolutionary process. Endorsing this historical phenomenon, Kautilya has designed his administrative machinery molded on the strong foundation of a centralized Monarchy. The quote justifies, "The King and his rule encapsulate [all] the constituents of the state" {Bk.8.Ch.2.Vs.1.}.

2) It has been an ever-proved historical fact that *Artha* (Resources of material well-being) is the most important constituent among the four constituents of *Purushartha*; such as *Dharma, Artha, Kama* and *Moksha*. The quote explains, "The source of the livelihood of men is *Artha* (Wealth); that is to say, the territory [and the inhabitants following various professions] is the wealth [of a nation]. The science by which territory is acquired and maintained [retained] is Arthashastra – the science of wealth and welfare" {Bk.15.Ch.1.Vs.1, 2.}. So Kautilya has mainly emphasized on the Acquisition of *Artha* (Resources of material well-being) by applying all available means. The basic theory Kautilya holds on for the Acquisition of *Artha* (Resources of material well-being) is *Prithvilabham* (Acquisition) and *Prithvipalanam* (Retention). Hence he believes in the enrichment and empowerment of the treasury of the state (*Kosha*).

3) It is quite natural that human beings are more subjective to emotions rather than reason. Naturally, human beings will lose their control over senses or emotions and they will be instigated for committing sins, crimes, imbalances; in response to the 'survival of the fittest' theory (*Matsyanaya*). According to Kautilya, uncompromising enactment of punishment *(Dhandaneethi)* is the only measure to control such commitment of sins, crimes, imbalances. "It is the power of punishment alone which, when exercised impartially in proportion to guilt and irrespective of whether the person punished is the King's son or the enemy, that protects this world and the next" {Bk.3.Ch.1Vs.42.}.

4) A sort of enemy attitude *(Ari Bhavam)* is latent within the human being as well as within the state. It cannot be nullified permanently through any sort of negotiations or treaties. If it seems to be nullified, it means that there will be a sound chance of its re-emergence after a short period of subsidence. Observing this natural and psychological phenomenon, Kautilya has established his theory of annihilating the enemy without leaving any room for its re-emergence. The implication of this absolute annihilation of enemy even extends to the extremity of public or secret assassination of the enemy. "An enemy's destruction shall be brought about even at the cost of great losses in men, material and wealth" {Bk.7.Ch.13.Vs.33.}. Ultimately this theory of annihilating the enemy results in *Prithvilabham* (Acquisition) and *Prithvipalanam* (Retention).

5) Kautilya strongly believe that the exposition of every administration should be free from religious fundamentalism, because the interference of religious fundamentalism in administration will generate anarchy in the state. The quote reads, "Because the King is the guardian of the right conduct of this world with its four *Varnas* and four *Ashramas*, he [alone] can enact and promulgate laws [to uphold them] when all traditional codes of conduct perish [through disuse or disobedience]." {Bk.3.Ch.1.Vs.38.}. Hence the statecraft as envisaged by Kautilya is free from religious fundamentalism.

"The three sciences [philosophy, the three Vedas and eco-
nomics] are dependent [for the development] on the science of government. [For, without a just administration, no
pursuit of learning or avocation would be possible]
[Government by] Rule of law, which alone can guarantee
security of life and the welfare of the people, is, in turn, dependent on [the] self-discipline [of the King]"

chapter-5

ARTHASHASTRA AND SOCIETY

It has been widely alleged by critics that Arthashastra lacks sufficient societal information and cultural landmarks of the period when it was composed. This is perhaps one of the most challenging allegations to unleash enough confusions on the date of composition and authorship of Arthashastra. This allegation is often defended or counter-argued by the fact that Arthashastra is basically a text on political sciences and for the same reason, not primarily concerned with the societal information and cultural landmarks of the period. Nevertheless it cannot avoid any reference to the social order and life prevailing in the society; for political life has no existence outside society.

The social order in Arthashastra is the *Four-Varna system* (*Chaturvarnya*) as observed in the *Smritis*. The *Four-Varna* oriented society or the *Aryagana* (The society of *Aryas*) is comprised of *Brahmin, Kshathriya, Vaishya* and *Sudra*. There are so many *Sub-Varna* clans such as *Chandala, Mlecha, Swapaka, Antavasayi, Pashanda, Pashandavasa* classified as *Anaryagana* (The society of *Non-Aryas*) and some other hill tribes such as *Adavika* and folk tribes such as *Baheerika* and *Dwarabaheerika*. Even then, the social order in Arthashastra when compared to later periods is very much reasonable and practical rather than superficial.

The core activities such as administration, learning, education and priesthood are assigned to the privileged upper class *Brahmins*. The army and other defense activities targeting *Prithvilabham* (Acquisition) are assigned to the *Kshathriyas*. Trade and commerce are assigned to the *Vaishyas*. Agriculture and Animal husbandry supplementing *Prithvipalanam* (Retention) are assigned to the *Sudras*. The Arthashastra elucidate the assignments of the *Chaturvarnya* as; "The duties of a *Brahmin* are: - study, teaching, performing the rituals prescribed for him, officiating at other people's rituals, giving and receiving gifts" {Bk.1.Ch.3.Vs.5}. "The duties of a *Kshathriya* are: - study, performing the rituals prescribed for him, living by [the profession of] arms and protecting all life" {Bk.1.Ch.3.Vs.6.}. "The duties of *Vaishyas* are: - study, performing the prescribed rituals, agriculture, cattle rearing and trade" {Bk.1.Ch.3.Vs.7.}. "The duties of a *Sudra* are: - service of the twice born [the three higher *Varnas*], [or] an economic activity [such as agriculture, cattle rearing and trade], [or] the profession of an artisan [or] and entertainer" {Bk.1.Ch.3.Vs.8.}.*Fig: 4.*

5.1. The emergence of an awakened Proletariat.

Later, with the emergence of Urbanization, the *Vaishyas* have migrated to the urban areas and they concentrated on more profit-generation from advanced trade and commerce activities in the urban belt. The *Sudras*; the proletariat at the same time worked as waged slaves in the land of *Vaishyas* throughout the year. The *Vaishyas*; in the meantime, have transformed themselves to petty bourgeoisie, the inevitable class-product of Urbanization; have begun to exploit the *Sudras*; the working class. The political thought of 'Sons of soil theory' gradually emerged in this historical moment. In the course of time a new revolutionary class has emerged and developed as a by-product of the class antagonism or the 'Sons of soil theory'. This revolutionary class known as *Kshudrakas*; can be called as the awakened proletariat and themselves positioned between the *Vaishyas* and the *Sudras*.

Lenin

The emergence of this awakened proletariat is the harbinger of the awakened proletariat incited by the Marxists in the later centuries. The social science of the emergence of this awakened proletariat is explained by V. I. Lenin: - "The proletariat seizes state power, and then transforms the means of production into state property. But in doing this, it puts an end to itself as the proletariat, it puts an end to all class differences and class antagonisms, it puts an end also to the state as the state. Former society, moving in class antagonisms, had need of the state, that is,

Figure: 4

```
                              ┌─────────┐
                              │ Society │
                              └────┬────┘
    ┌────────┬────────────┬────────┼────────┬─────────────┐
┌────────┐ ┌────────┐ ╭──────────╮ ┌──────────┐ ┌────────┐
│Brahmin │ │ Vaisya │ │ King's   │ │Kshatriya │ │ Sudra  │
└───┬────┘ └───┬────┘ │Monarchical│ └────┬─────┘ └───┬────┘
              │      │ and      │
┌─────────┐ ┌────────┐│ Paternal │ ┌──────────┐ ┌──────────┐
│Physical │ │ Trade  ││ Control  │ │ National │ │Agriculture│
│and      │ │ and    │╰────┬─────╯ │ Defence  │ │and       │
│spiritual│ │Commerce│ ╭─────────╮ └──────────┘ │Animal    │
│Admn.    │ └────────┘ │ Economy │              │Husbandry │
└─────────┘            │ Artha   │              └──────────┘
                       ╰────┬────╯
              ┌──────────────────────┐
              │ Prithvilabham        │
              │ Prithvipalanam       │
              └──────────┬───────────┘
                  ╭───────────────╮
                  │ Yogakshemam   │     The Structure of Society
                  │ Welfare State │        in Arthashastra
                  ╰───────────────╯
```

The Structure of Society in Arthashastra

an organization of the exploiting class at each period for the maintenance of its external conditions of production; therefore, in particular, for the forcible holding down of the exploited class in the conditions of oppression (slavery, bondage or serfdom, waged -labour) determined by the existing mode of production. The state was the official representative of society as a whole, its embodiment in a visible corporate body; but it was this only in so far as it was the state of that class which itself in its epoch, represented society as a whole: in ancient times, the state of the slave owning citizens; in the Middle Ages, of the feudal nobility; in our epoch, of the bourgeoisie". (V. I. Lenin, State and Revolution, New York: International Publishers Co., Inc., 1932),

5.2. The society of yeomanry and welfare state.

Arthashastra has planned for a welfare state of benefited living. It also advocated the philosophy of sustenance of Livelihood that synchronizes with the theory of *Prithvilabham* (Acquisition) and *Prithvipalanam* (Retention). The *Shastras* that hold on the Philosophy of sustenance of livelihood, and theory of *Prithvilabham* (Acquisition) and *Prithvipalanam* (Retention) are to refrain from physical as well as psychological sort of injury and other evils; but adhere to truthfulness, purity, universal love and forgiveness. "While gifts of money can assuage the pain of the darts of speech, destroying property means depriving another of his livelihood" {Bk.8.Ch.3.Vs.23-29.}. "No one would want to lose his own life even for a large sum of money. [In any case,] One who inflicts physical injury is likely to suffer the same fate from others" {Bk.8.Ch.3.Vs.30-36.}.

It is a society that duly respected the *Chaturvarnya* system and solemnly observed all the rites and rituals attached to the Vedic science. It is a society that is fully subservient to a strong centralized Monarchy and showed no signs of resistance or resentment against the Monarch. "Without a King, there will only be the law of the jungle, subjects who do not pay fines and taxes take on themselves the sins of Kings, while Kings who do not look after the welfare of the people take on themselves the sins of the subjects. Kings shall never be insulted because divine punishment will be visited on whoever slights them. Thus people shall be discouraged from having seditious thoughts" {Bk.1.Ch.13.Vs.4 -13.}. This subservient relationship of the subjects to the Monarch is beautifully explained in the *Sri Chanakya Neetishastra; The Political Ethics of Chanakya Pandit* (Raja Ram Kumar Press, Lucknow, 1981) translated by Miles Davis: "If the king is virtuous, then the subjects are also virtuous. If the king is sinful, then the subjects also become sinful. If he is mediocre, then the subjects are mediocre. The subjects follow the example of the king. In short, as is the king so are the subjects". {Ch.13.Vs.8}.

It is a society of yeomanry limited to middle class enjoyments and developed a sort of frozen impassiveness towards the political events. This submissiveness and impassiveness is the by-product of the three dominant sciences (philosophy, the three *Vedas* and economics) on which the society was structured. "The three sciences [philosophy, the three Vedas and economics] are dependent [for the development] on the science of government. [For, without a just administration, no pursuit of learning or avocation would be possible] [Government by] Rule of law, which alone can guarantee security of life and the welfare of the people, is, in turn, dependent on [the] self-discipline[of the King]" {Bk.1.Ch.5.Vs.1-2.}. In other words it can be undoubtedly concluded that it is the Monarch who has deliberately developed such a kind of submissiveness and impassiveness in the subjects. This purposeful contrivance of the enforced submissiveness and impassiveness on people enabled them to tolerate and overcome the social injustice, inequality, evils and *Adharma* (Unlawful activities).

5.3. **Dharma** *and Marital relationship.*

Arthashastra emphasize strong and practical marital relationships; for it is one among the frontline shields that defends the Kautilyan state, its culture and moral science and save them from all the threats and tendencies of deviations from the normal standards of life. Considering the superior *varna* of husband and wife, marriages are generaly divided into two : 1. *Anuloma* Marriage 2. *Partiloma* Marriage. *Fig. : 5.*

There are eight types of marriage in Arthashastra under two classifications known as *Dharmya* and *Adharmya*. This classification is based upon the approval and disapproval of the father of the bride. *Dharmya* marriages consists of four types such as *Brahma, Prajapatya, Aarhsa* and *Daiva*; all ceremonious marriages with the approval of the father. *Adharmya* marriages

Figure: 5

***Anuloma / Pratiloma* Marriage**

		Varna of WIFE			
		Brahmin	Kshatriya	Vaishya	Sudra
		Anuloma marriage - Husband of superior varna			
Varna of HUSBAND	Brahmin		Brahmin	Ambastha	Nishada Parasava
	Kshatriya	Suta		Kshatriya	Ugra
	Vaishya	Vaidehaka	Magadha	Sudra	
	Sudra	Chandala	Kshatta	Ayogava	
		Pratiloma marriages - wife of superior varna			

that are unceremonious marriages without the approval of the father, consists of four types such as *Gandharva, Aasura, Rakshasa* and *Paisacha*. "With the approval of the women's father, the first (*Dharmya*), four become *Dharmya* [lawful and sacred]. The latter (*Adharmya*), four become lawful [only] with the approval of the father and the mother [of the women]" {Bk.3.Ch.2.Vs.2-10.}.

According to Kautilya, marriage is the source of all social evils and disputes. He has given a detailed commentary on the eight types of marriages in the third *Adhikarana* of Arthashastra: "Marriage is the basis of all disputes. The giving in marriage of a virgin well-adorned is called "*Brahma*-marriage." The joint performance of sacred duties by a man and a woman is known as "*Prajapatya*-marriage." The giving in marriage of a virgin for a couple of cows is called "*Arsha* -marriage." The giving in marriage of a virgin to an officiating priest in a sacrifice is called "*Daiva*-marriage." The voluntary union of a virgin with her lover is called "*Gandharva*-marriage." Giving a virgin after receiving plenty of wealth is termed "*Aasura*-marriage." The abduction of a virgin is called "*Rakshasa*-marriage." The abduction of a virgin while she is still asleep and intoxicated is called "*Paisacha*-marriage." Of these, the first four [*Dharmya*] are ancestral customs of old and are valid on their being approved of by the father. The rest [*Adharmya*] are to be sanctioned by both the father and the mother; for it is they that receive the money paid by the bridegroom for their daughter. In case of the absence by death of either the father or the mother, the survivor will receive the money-payment. If both of them are dead, the virgin herself shall receive it. Any kind of marriage is approvable, provided it pleases all those that are concerned in it." (*Kautilya, Kautilya's Arthashastra*, 2d Ed., trans. R. Shamashastry (Mysore: Wesleyan Mission Press, 1923), passim.).

It is also worth commenting that the penal code in Arthashastra provides a very dominant lead-role for the code of marital relationships (*Vivahasamyuktham*) among the 17 laws in the penal code. The chronology of the Arthashastra code of laws is: (1) *Vivahasamyuktham* (Marriage and allied topics) (2) *Dhayavibhagam* (Partition of inheritance) (3) *Vasthukam* (Properties and disputes concerning it) (4) *Samayanapakarmam* (Failure to participate in community affairs) (5) *Hrunadhanam* (Non-payment of debts) (6) *Aupanidhikam* (Concerning deposits) (7) *Dasakarmakarakalpam* (Laws concerning slaves and labourers) (8) *Sambuyasamuthanam* (Undertakings in partnerships) (9) *Vikreetakritanusayam* (Revocation of a sale or a purchase) (10) *Dathanapakarmam* (Non-conveyance of gifts made) (11) *Aswamivikrayam* (Sale without ownership) (12) *Saswamisam-bandham* (Laws concerning ownership) (13) *Sahasam* (Forcible seizure of an object) (14) *Vakparushyam* (Verbal injury) (15) *Dhandaparushyam* (Physical injury) (16) *Dhuthasamahwayam* (Gambling and challenging) (17) *Prakeernakas* (Miscell-aneous). All the cases especially civil cases are investigated and heard in the light of marital relationship of the involved. "[An examination of] civil transactions begin with marriage" {Bk.3.Ch.2.Vs.1.}. According to L.N. Rangarajan, the role of the *Grihasta* - householder - is an important stage in every Arya's life because it is during this period that a man contributes to economic activity and maintenance of social order, particularly the perpetuation of his family line. Prof. R.P. Kangle also comments that the Kautilya's code of marital relationship is of a most rational kind.

5.4. Women Participation in Arthashastra.

Women in Arthashastra have been provided with ample freedom, dominance and active participation in the administrative system without any discrimination over gender, colour or *Varna* scheme. Arthashastra allows widow remarriage and right to divorce, sabotaging the deep -rooted conventions enwrapped in fabricated or biased laws in the *Smritis.* "A widow without sons, who remains faithful to her [deceased] husband's bed, shall enjoy, to the end of her life, her property, under the protection of the elders [of the husband's family]. {Bk.3.Ch.2.Vs.19.}. "If a widow remarries after receiving all the above, she shall forfeit what was left to her by her [previous] husband and shall also be obliged to return the rest with inter- est" {Bk.3.Ch.2.Vs.20.}. Women have also been provided with dignified professional status in the society through employing them in the Department of Espionage, Income Tax, Defense and in the Bureau of Intelligence of the state. Arthashastra quotes, "Inside the city, they [Women as spies] shall search deserted houses, workshops, drinking places, vegetarian and non-vegetarian eating houses, gambling places and the quarters of heretics". {Bk.2.Ch.36.Vs.13-14.}. "watch shall be kept over those who spend lavishly and those doing so in drinking houses without hav- ing known source of income". {Bk.2.Ch.25.Vs.6.}.

Employment opportunities are also opened to them in the areas of agriculture as agricultur- al workers; in the areas of textile industry as weavers and spinners; in the areas of civil service as attendants; in the areas of breweries as blenders of alcohol; and in the areas of entertain- ments as *Ganikas* [prostitutes with a social cause and stature; for increasing revenue and for detecting crimes] or entertainers. Unlike *Smritis* Arthashastra entertains a free vision and inno- vative perspective on women as dignified individual, class and society and accordingly there emerged a new social order that respecting and serving the fellow community.

"The root of wealth is [economic] activity and lack of it [brings] material distress. In the absence of [fruitful economic] activity, both current prosperity and future growth are in danger of destruction. A King can achieve the desired objectives and abundance of riches by undertaking [productive] economic activity"

chapter-8

ARTHASHASTRA AND INDIAN ECONOMICS

Arthashastra has theorized a practical Finance Management Science that even today agrees with the fundamentals of modern finance management principles. Hence, Arthashastra has been considered to be the foremost and authoritative book on Finance Management ever written in the history. Kautilya correlates all activities in the state with money-generation (*Artha*). "All activities depend first on the treasury [*Artha*]. Therefore, a King shall devote his best attention to it" {Bk.2.Ch.8.Vs.1, 2.}.

According to Arthashastra, administrative efficiency and practicality are the most important prerequisites needed for any financial Management system. If these two factors are lacking in the finance Management system, it will destroy the current prosperity and the future development of the state. "The root of wealth is [economic] activity and lack of it [brings] material distress. In the absence of [fruitful economic] activity, both current prosperity and future growth are in danger of destruction. A King can achieve the desired objectives and abundance of riches by undertaking [productive] economic activity" {Bk.1.Ch.19.Vs.35-36.}. This is the basic philosophy on which Arthashastra has theorized its practical diversified economy.

Arthashastra aims at an absolute profit-based economic system. According to Kautilya, money *(Artha)* is the only available device that can make more money *(Artha)*. "Just as elephants are needed to catch elephants, so does one need wealth to capture more wealth" {Bk.9.Ch.4.Vs.27.}. So it has to be the dire need of the state to mobilize money *(Artha)* by all means. Here, the mobilization of money *(Artha)* or the resources that supplement the material well-being exactly implies the basic theory of *Prithvilabham* (Acquisition) [of *Artha* or wealth] and *Prithvipalanam* (Retention) [of *Artha* or wealth] in Arthashastra. It means that without wealth, there is no production or acquisition and if there is no production or acquisition, then, there will not be any acquired resources to retain. So Kautilya insists upon the mobilization of maximum wealth by applying all available means. This philosophy is very clear from the *Sloka* cited from *Chanakyasutra*.

Sarvascha sampadha: sarvopayena parigraheth

Chanakyasutra, Chapter-2, Sutra-20

The theory of economics in Arthashastra has formulated a well stabilized, integrated and a balanced Finance Management System. It mobilized maximum (*Artha*) material resources through the three-fold economic activity termed as *Vartha*; comprised of agriculture, animal husbandry and trade and commerce. "Agriculture, cattle rearing and trade constitute economic activity. They are the main sources of wealth- i.e. grains, cattle, gold, forest produce and labour. The king obtains through them the treasury and the army, which [are then used to] bring under control both his own people and the enemy's people." {Bk.1.Ch.4.Vs.1-2.}. According to Kautilya, the state will be like a barren cow if its *Janapada* (country side) do not have the three-fold economic activity termed as *Vartha*. "For power comes from the countryside, which is the source of all [economic] activities" {Bk.7.Ch.14. Vs.19.} One could experience the essence of Gandhian Philosophy and Economics in these Kautilyan quotes.

Arthashastra has developed an economic theory; a synthesis of fine-tuned Agricultural Economics, Pastoral Economics and Industrial Economics based on *Vartha*, the three-fold economic activity formulated by Kautilya. Gradually, there emerged an integrated form of Agro-Pastoral economics in general and in latter periods; it streamlined an Industrial economics as a total economic solution to preserve the people's welfare. The four sectors of manufacturing industry that made Industrial Economics concrete are state monopolies such as mining for making weapons *(Dhanda)* and brewing liquor *(Sura)*, state controlled industries such as textiles *(Sutra)*, salt *(Lavana)* and jewelry *(Suvarna)*, state regulated small scale industries of craftsmen such as goldsmith, blacksmith, weavers and dyers and unregulated craftsmen like potters, basket makers etc.

This rudimentary economic equation is perfectly controlled by five important constituents namely (i) King, (ii) Ministers, (iii) Treasury *(Kosa)*, (iv) Country *(Janapada)* and (v) Army *(Dhanda)*. Among the five constituents treasury *(Kosa)* is considered to be the core constituent. It is the powerful Treasury *(Kosa)* that ensures people's acquisition of welfare *(Prithvilabham)* and retention of the acquired welfare *(Prithvipalanam)*. The Kautilyan dictum is 'from wealth *(Kosa)* comes the power of the government *(Dhanda)*. *Dhanda* also implies weapon or army. With the treasury and the army *(Kosadhanda)*, the earth is acquired with the treasury as the ornament'. "The source of the financial strength of the state is the mining [and metallurgical] industry; the state exercises power because of its treasury. With [increased] wealth and a [powerful] army more territory can be acquired, thereby further increasing the wealth of the state" {Bk.2.Ch.12.Vs.37.}.

Kautilya cautioned all sections in the *Janapada* for not to deplete the treasury by any means. For depletion of treasury will make one bankrupt and in turn destroys the very vitality or welfare of the citizens and the country. "A King with a depleted treasury eats into the very vitality of the citizens and the country" {Bk.2.Ch.1.Vs.16.}. Hence, the circumstance that leads to the depletion of treasury has been seriously dealt in Arthashastra. The king imposed heavy penalty and punishments on those who incurred loss to the state by any means. Considering the quantum of loss incurred, Kautilya classified such people as *Thadathvika* (Those who destroy their own wealth), *Moolahara* (Those who destroy the paternal wealth) and *Kadharya* (Those who accumulate wealth from the home country and invest in foreign treasury). Such people according to Kautilya are swallowing or nullifying the King's wealth, Kingdom and its Workers [human resources]. "He who causes loss of revenue swallows the Kings wealth, he who produce double the [anticipated] revenue eats up the country [kingdom] and he who spends all the revenue [without bringing in any profit] swallows the labour of workers [human resources]" {Bk.2.Ch.9.Vs.13, 15, 17.}.

Kautilya is the first Indian economist who found that the Indian Economics is based on its geography and agriculture. The value of the land is determined by its productive agricultural outputs (Products) and the *Sudra* farming community or collective human resource inputs (People) involved. "The value of land is what man makes of it" {Bk.7.Ch.11.Vs.9.}. The land has been divided into regions for dry crops and wet crops. "in regions where cultivation is dependent solely on the rain; land is classified as suitable for dry crops, if the rainfall is about sixteen *Dronas* [about 25 inches] a year; and for wet crops, if the rainfall is one and half times that [about 37 ½ inches a year]." {Bk.2.Ch.24.Vs.5.}. The rainy season of the time has been clearly marked as per the available observatory mechanism of the time. It is a remarkable fact that this observation procedure agrees to the modern Agro Meteorology Observatory System. "A good rainy season is one when one third of the annual rainfall occurs at the beginning (*Sravana* – July/August) and at the end of the season (*Kartika* – October/ November) and two thirds in the middle (*praushtapada* – August/September and *Asvayuja* – September Octo-ber)" {Bk.2.Ch.24.Vs.7.}.

Mauryan Coin

6.1. Agricultural Economics and Water Management.

The preservation and management of water resources has been given a prominent role in the Kautilya's Agro-Economics. The water management has its specific work areas such as preservation, control, development and distribution. In Arthashastra, the right to property related to water resources and control over water resources is vested upon the king or the state. "No one shall let water out of dams out of turn; No one shall obstruct, through negligence, the [rightful] use of water by others; No one shall obstruct a customary water course in use; No one shall make a customary water course unusable [by diverting the water]; No one shall build a dam or a well on land belonging to someone else or; No one shall sell or mortgage, directly or indirectly, a bund or embankment built and long used as a charitable public undertaking except when it is in ruins or has been abandoned." {Bk.3.Ch.9.Vs.38.}, {Bk.3.Ch.10. Vs.1-2.}.

However, for encouraging new entrepreneurs for the construction and management of new reservoirs or irrigation projects, privatization of such projects are also entertained under certain conditions. "Waterworks such as reservoirs, embankments and tanks can be privately owned and the owner shall be free to sell or mortgage them. The ownership of tanks shall lapse, if they had not been in use for a period of five years, except in cases of distress. Any one leasing, hiring, sharing or accepting a water works as a pledge, with the right to use them, shall keep them in good condition." {Bk.3.Ch.9.Vs.34, 32, 36.}. In order to encourage privatization, tax exemptions for three to five years are also granted to those private entrepreneurs involved in the construction of new tanks and embankments; renovation of ruined or abandoned water works; and cleaning of water works over-grown with weeds.

The entire natural and man-made water resources and the nearby lands and its agro-aquatic resources are state properties. The government is very much responsible for the growth and development of the water resources both natural and man-made, for facilitating irrigation and drinking water distribution to the people. Water resources management projects are implemented with the co-operative efforts of the people. Those who refuse to co-operate in such ventures are compulsorily made to share the cost of project without giving them the benefits of such projects as a part of punishment. Natural water resources are protected and preserved. "Dams built to store water from a flowing source [such as rain or a river] are preferable to those built to store water brought by canals [i.e. dug for the purpose]. Among reservoirs built by damming rivers, the one which irrigates a larger area is better." {Bk.7.Ch.12.Vs.4-5.}. "He [the king] shall build storage reservoirs, [filling them] either from natural springs or with water brought from elsewhere; or, he may provide help to those who build reservoirs by giving them land, building roads and channels or giving grants of timber and implements". {Bk.2.Ch.1.Vs.20-21.}.

The strategic management of these Dams and reservoirs can be considered as the pioneer successful projects on Water Management Systems and Rain water harvesting projects of the modern times. There was clear indication of the organized irrigation projects by the villages in the absence of anyone responsible to initiate such projects. "In the absence of the owner, either charitable individuals or the people of village acting together, shall maintain water works." {Bk.3.Ch.10.Vs.3.}. Besides, there is a strong reference to the value-addition and preservation of rain water in the *Sri Chanakya Neetishastra; The Political Ethics Of Chanakya Pandit* (Raja Ram Kumar Press, Lucknow, 1981) translated and edited by Miles Davis; "Rain which falls upon the sea is useless; so is food for one who is satiated; in vain is a gift for one who is wealthy; and a burning lamp during the daytime is useless. There is no water like rainwater; no strength like one's own; no light like that of the eyes; and no wealth dearer than food grain". {Ch.5.16-17}. This valuable thinking poesy on value-addition and preservation of rain water and other source of natural water, has either been made to dormant due to the severe lack of the we-feeling or delayed due to the crippled approach of our modern environmentalists or water management experts. However, the new village-based rain water and natural water preservation movements are now initiated by some foreseers of its kind; such as *Jalanidhi* or *Jalasakthi* movements of today are really encouraging and in fact highly indebted to the great environmentalist Kautilya.

6.2. Sacramental approach to Agriculture.

Agriculture has been made a statutory economic activity. Liberalized tax policies, encouragements through subsidies and motivations given to the agriculturists accelerated the growth and development of agriculture. Arthashastra protects agriculture from being hindered or harassed by the oppressive forces of taxes and the lack of ample labour or human resources. "He [the king] shall protect agriculture from being harassed by [onerous] fines, taxes and demands for labour" {Bk.2.Ch.1.Vs.37.}. "Anyone who brings new land under cultivation shall be granted exemption from payment of agricultural taxes for a period of two years" {Bk.3.Ch.9.Vs.33.}. No one is allowed to waste his land uncultivated; heavy penalty has been imposed on such people. "The loss suffered by the state due to non-cultivation shall be made good by the offending holder" {Bk.2.Ch.1.Vs.9.}. "The settlers in the villages shall mainly be *Sudra* agriculturists, with a minimum of one hundred families and a maximum of five hundred. The villages shall be sited so as to provide mutual protection" {Bk.2.Ch.1.Vs.2.}. The *Sudras* who have been engaged in agriculture are paid wages either in cash or in kind in accordance with a need-based economy considering the market conditions.

The Agro-Economic society set up by Kautilya in the Indo-Ganges is an organized society. It is the King, the mastermind behind this organized society, who enforced a socio-economic discipline among the people and society. *Fig: 6.* "The King shall enforce the laws regarding discipline among members of a family, slaves and persons mortgaged' {Bk.2.Ch.1.Vs.25.}. The multi-purpose tool he applied for the framing of this Agro-Economic society is *Vartha;* (The three-fold economic activity consists of agriculture, animal husbandry and trade and commerce) of which the dominant component is agriculture. The economic stability and integrity of this Agro-Economic society has been vigilantly monitored and safeguarded by the *Sitadhyaksha* (The chief superintendent of crown lands/agriculture). *Sitadhyaksha* is the most important *Adhyaksha* (Chief Superintendent) among the 34 heads of departments in Arthashastra. He should be highly skilled and conversant with all the sciences of agriculture and cultivation. He is responsible for the seed collection, land preparation, seed preparation and sowing, manure application and plant protection, proper harvesting and threshing, organizing the labour or human resources, leasing out for cultivation and water resource management.

It is the moral responsibility of the *Sitadhyaksha* (The chief superintendent of crown lands/ agriculture) to promote the spirit of agriculture and also to keep the culture and tradition of the *Janapada* in all fields of agriculture. No foreign forces are allowed either to intervene or to transform the agricultural tradition of the country. It is indeed a paradox that it took another 2300 years to endorse this strategic economic fact by the Indian economists. Satish. Y. Deodar has endorsed the fact that India should essentially prefer incrementing the agricultural production to initiating the phases of liberalization. His study has also proved that the aggregate means of domestic support of all developing countries including India are declining to a negative trend. (*Implications of WTO agreements for Indian agriculture*, CMA, IIM, 2001). The most praiseworthy factor in Arthashastra is that agriculture has been honoured as an indispensable sacrament and cultivation as a sacramental ritual. "The chief superintendent [of crown lands/agriculture] shall decide on the sowing of wet crops, dry crops or summer crops according to the water available, the nature of the land and the season. He shall have the seeds prepared as prescribed. Whenever a crop is sown for the first time [in a season], he shall take a handful of seed soaked in a pot of water containing gold, and sow it after reciting the *mantra*:

Salutations to Lord Prajapati Kasyapa!

Let the crops flourish always!

Let the goddess reside in the seeds and the grains!"

{Bk.2.Ch.24.Vs.11, 15, 19, 23, 27.}

6.3. Arthashastra and Finance Management.

It is very interesting to note the fact that even the penal code in Arthashastra is a valuable contributory component of the financial code that generates the revenue of the state and that strengthens the treasury *(Kosa)*. The judiciary is also made to function in such a way as to contribute resources to the treasury through the recovery of monetary fines and ransom against freedom from physical punishments. Monetary fines were of three kinds: *Dhanda* (Fines levied by Heads of departments), *Athyaya* (Fines levied by judges and magistrates) and *Ayuktadhanda* (Fines paid by government servants). Almost all physical punishments pronounced by the judiciary in Arthashastra can be compensated by *Artha* [or material resources] or by *Vishti* [labour] against the equal value of the punishments as fixed by the court. In the same manner tax can also be remitted either by way of money or by way of material resources such as grain, gold, cattle, forest produce or even as labour or human resources *(Vishti)* as *Pratikara* (compensation to tax).

The efficiency of the Finance Management in Arthashastra is not determined by the acquisition and retention of the resources alone. It also ensures a very good equilibrium of social security, agro-industrial production, crisis management and human resource management. "Ensuring the prosperity of the state, continuing of successful financial policies, eliminating thefts, keeping strict control over the government employees, increasing agriculture production, promoting trade [and commerce], avoiding troubles and calamities, reducing [tax] exemptions and remissions and increasing cash income are the means of increasing the wealth of the state" {Bk.2.Ch.8.Vs.3.}

Kautilya was very vigilant on the proper maintenance of accounting and auditing. He never allowed any sort of loss of revenue to the state or any criminal tendencies either to obstruct or to misuse the wealth of the state. "Obstruction, misuse of government property and false accounting by government servants lead to a reduction of wealth" {Bk.2.Ch.8.Vs.4.}. Kautilya employs spies to investigate the reasons for the loss of revenue in all public activities. "The loss caused [due to inadequate supervision] by fellow officials, sureties, subordinates, sons, brothers, wife, daughters and servants [the one later in the list] becoming liable [if an earlier one fails to compensate]" {Bk.2.Ch.7.Vs.5.} Receipts and expenditure of the state are well monitored and the rules and procedures of the financial year are also maintained. "If receipts and expenditure are properly looked after the King will not find himself in financial difficulties" {Bk.5.Ch.3.Vs.45.} The financial year was set to the lunar calendar. "The closing day for the accounting year shall be the full moon day of the month of *Ashada* (June-July) , the year consisting of 354 days (According to the lunar calendar) with a separate book for intercalary month" {Bk.2.Ch.7.Vs.6-8, 16.}. "On the closing day for accounts, all accounts officers [of the regions, undertakings etc.] shall present themselves with sealed account books and with the [net] balance [of revenue over expenditure] in sealed containers. The officers shall be kept separate and shall not be allowed to talk [to each other]" {Bk.2.Ch.7.Vs.17.}.

The multiplicity of taxation in Arthashastra has created wide criticism. However, the prompt collection of taxes in Arthashastra has been highly applauded. Taxes are but the major driving force behind the successful administration of the state. According to Kautilya taxes are existential necessity of a natural phenomenon. Taxes are to be collected when people are strong enough to pay the taxes. "Just as one plucks fruits from a garden as they ripen, so shall a King have the revenue collected as it becomes due. Just as one does not collect unripe fruits, he shall avoid taking wealth that is not due because that will make the people angry and spoil the very sources of revenue" {Bk.5.Ch.2.Vs.70.}. The tax structure in Arthashastra is based on the above -mentioned metaphoric economic philosophy and vision. But in times of economic crisis of the state, this economic Philosophy and vision are seen to have been either violated or made flexible. In such crisis situations, heavy taxation policies with compulsory or even militaristic recovery pattern are imposed. Considering the contingencies of the crisis Management, such imposition of taxes is to be tolerated or justified.

There are a number of ways in Arthashastra by which the gullibility of the public has been exploited to collect money in times of crisis. This includes building overnight, as if it happened by a miracle, a temple or a sanctuary and promoting the holding of fairs and festivals in honors of the miraculous deity; using secret agents to frighten people into making offerings to drive away an evil spirit; playing tricks on people by showing a cobra apparently with many heads, or a stone cobra coming alive; and selling remedies against evil occult manifestations. {Bk.5.Ch.2.Vs.39-45.}. If we examine the various cross sections of the society around the globe, we may be able to see such types of exploitations in its modern hi-tech behaviour or multinational dimensions. "The chief superintendent of temples shall collect together the wealth of temples in the city and in the countryside. Then, [using a similar pretext] the property shall be taken away to the treasury]" {Bk.5.Ch.2.Vs.37-38.}. The other ways of exploitations of public wealth for the state are: selling of favours, honours and status to the rich and expropriating temple property. "The King may also ask the rich to give as much gold as they can either voluntarily or in expectation of favours. Honours and status symbols (Umbrella, Headgear, decorations) may be bestowed on them return for gold" {Bk.5.Ch.2.Vs.35-36.}.

6.4. Budgeting in Arthashastra.

On closely observing the theory of revenue budgeting in Arthashastra, it is very clear that the budgeting procedure of the modern times has nothing to claim as modern, but it can be even alleged that it is far away from the proven economic concepts of Arthashastra. There are seven main heads of account for the main body of revenue accounts *(Ayasareeram)* and seven sub heads for the main heads of revenue accounts *(Ayamukham)* Fig: 7, 8, 9 & 10. Besides, the revenue collected by the chief superintendent of warehouse *(Koshtagaradhayksha)*, the revenue accumulated as savings from expenditure *(Vyayapratyam)* and the revenue flow in the form of tax collected by way of cash or kind and the value of labour utilized by human resources *(Vishti)* also supplements the revenue. "Actual income is to be calculated under the headings- (i) Current income; (ii) Transferred income and (iii) Miscellaneous revenue" {Bk.2.Ch.6.Vs.17.}. "Actual expenditure shall be shown under the headings- (i) Budgeted day to day expenditure, (ii) Unbudgeted day to day expenditure and (iii) Foreseen periodic (Fortnightly, Monthly or Annual) expenditure" {Bk.2.Ch.6.Vs.23-26.}. "The net revenue is to be calculated after deducting expenditure from income, taking into account the actual as well as deferred amounts" {Bk.2.Ch.6.Vs.27.}. There are departmental or regional accounts officers engaged for the proper maintenance, submission and auditing of the accounts. 'All accounts shall be maintained in the proper form and legibly written without corrections. Failure to do so shall be a punishable offence' {Bk.2.Ch.7.Vs.35.}. 'Day to day accounts [to be submitted once a month] shall be presented before the end of the following month and late submission shall be penalized' {Bk.2.Ch.7.Vs.26-27.}. 'An auditor shall be ready when an accounts officer presents himself for audit; otherwise, he shall be punished' {Bk.2.Ch.7.Vs.22.}. Manipulation of accounts through forging lies and fabricating contradictions by any officer will invite highest level standard penalty. "High officials shall be responsible for rendering the accounts in full for their sphere of activity without any contradiction in them. Those who tell lies or make contradictory statements shall pay the highest level standard penalty" {Bk.2.Ch.7.Vs.25.}. The tax structure and the accounting concepts are given in Fig. 7.

Figure: 6

A Hypothetical Kautilyan State

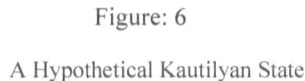

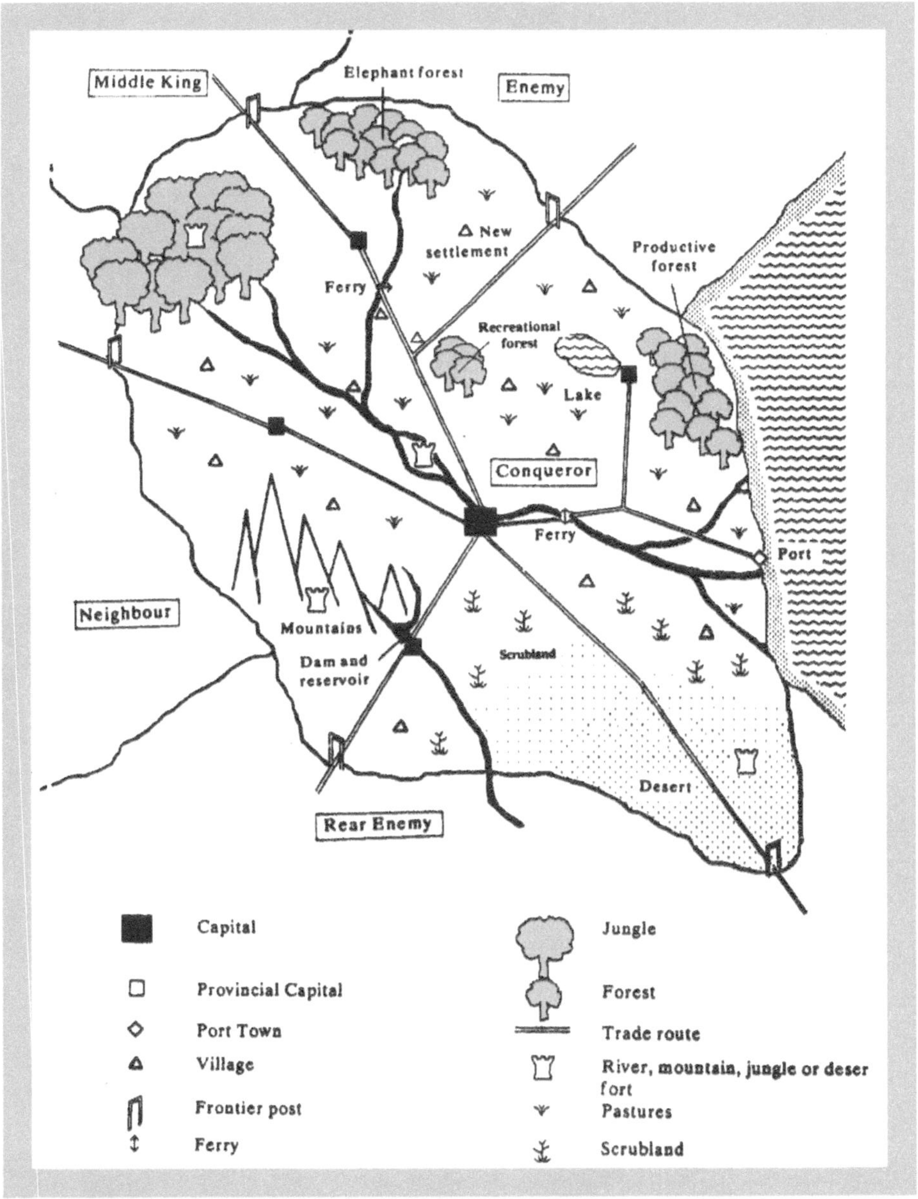

Figure : 7

TAX STRUCTURE IN ARTHASHASTRA

Sl.No.	Original Terminology	Modern Terminology with details
1	Sulkam	Customs duty a) Import duty b) Export duty c) Octroi & taxes
2	Vyaji	Transaction Tax a) on Crown goods
3	Bhagham	Share of production a) 1/6th of production
4	Karam	Tax in cash
5	Prathikaram	Tax in kind
6	Vydharanam	Counterveiling duties or tax
7	Varthani	Road cess
8	Parigham	Monopoly tax
9	Prakrayam	Royalty
10	Pindakaram	Tax paid in kind from villages
11	Senabaktham	Army maintenance tax
12	Parswam	Surcharges

Figure : 8

TAX STRUCTURE IN ARTHASHASTRA

\(Ayashareeram\) Main bodies of revenue/income		
Sl.No.	Original Terminology	Modern Terminology with details
1	Dhurgam	Fortified town
2	Rashtram	Country side
3	Ghani	Mines
4	Sethu	Irrigation projects
5	Vanam	Forest
6	Vrajam	Animal husbandry
7	Vanikpadam	Trade
\(Ayamukham\) Main heads of revenue/income		
Sl.No.	Original Terminology	Modern Terminology with details
1	Mulyam	Cost price
2	Bhagham	Share
3	Parigham	Monopoly tax
4	Kliptham	Fixed charges
5	Roopikam	Manufacturing charges
6	Athyayam	Fine & Penalities
7	Vyaji	Transaction tax

Figure : 9

TAX STRUCTURE IN ARTHASHASTRA

(Ayam) Other sources of revenue/income		
Sl.No.	Original Terminology	Modern Terminology with details
1	Revenue collected by the Koshtagaradhyakshan	Revenue collected by the Chief superintendent of warehouse
2	Vyayaprathyanga	Savings from expenditure
3	Ayudheeyam	Revenue collected through the Administrator
4	Prathikaram	Tax collected as cash or kind
5	Revenue collected through Japthi	Confiscated kinds
6	Revenue collected by Sthanika & Gopan	Revenue collected through the Governor and Record keeper
7	Prakeernaka	Miscellaneous sources of Revenue/Income

Figure : 10

TAX STRUCTURE IN ARTHASHASTRA

(Vyayam) Main bodies of expenditure	
Sl.No.	Main body with details
1	Worship and Charity
2	Palace
3	Administration
4	Foreign Affairs
5	Manufacturing
6	Labour or Human Resources
7	Granary, Ordinance, Depot and Stores
8	Defence
9	Pastures/Cattle
10	Forest and foerst reserved for the king's entertainments
11	Fuel and fodder
12	Gifts and honours

"A King can reign only with the help of others,
one wheel alone does not move. Therefore,
a King should appoint advisers [*Mahamatras*]
and listen to their advice"

chapter-7

THE PHILOSOPHY OF HRD AND ARTHASHASTRA

I t is very evident that Kautilya with his foresight and insight has formulated his own strategic economic policies that interlinked with the human resource development policies. This interlink has finally resulted in the idea of economic liberalization. The Philosophy of Human Resource Development (HRD) and the science of economic liberalization have ideologically synthesized later. Dr. P. Subba Rao has described this synthesis as follows: - "HRD assumes significance in view of the fast changing organizational environments and need of the organization to adopt new techniques in order to respond to the environmental changes. The changing environmental factors include: unprecedented increase in competition within and outside the country consequent upon the announcement and implementation of economic liberalizations." It is this Strategy of Human Resource Development (HRD) that enables the society to overcome such unprecedented increase in competitive trends. It is this scientific Human Resource Planning (HRP) that capacitates the society for this task and the capacity will work in the present as well as in the future.

In the modern context, where the role of HRD has been considered as decisive in the process of enhancing the efficiency of Administration and Management; the practical administrative solutions as envisaged in Arthashastra are remarkably relevant. It can also be proved that those practical administrative solutions have the nature of a successful continuum from the past to present.

The Philosophy of Human Resource Development (HRD) is nowadays widely discussed among the Gurus of modern administration and management who are still exploring the unfathomable possibilities of human resource management in their management school laboratories. The ultimate aim of this book therefore is to explain the practical application of HRD in the context of Kautilyan philosophy, in the areas of administration and management of the simple organizations to the compound and complex organizations in the state or nation.

It is believed that Leonard Naddler was the first management thinker who drafted the concept of Human Resource Development (HRD). He had introduced the concept through the research paper he presented in the American Society for Training and Development during 1969. He has defined Human Resource Development (HRD) as "those learning experiences which are organized, for a specific time, and designed to bring about the possibility of behavioral change". This primary definition of Naddler is but a blank statement of an earlier interpreter of the colonial administration. Later, this blank statement on management thought along with its aftershocks has been imposed on the global management community.

The concept of Human Resource Development (HRD) formulated by Naddler, has confronted many transitions later and finally reached the active arena of innovative educational methods, sociological developments and observations of behavioral science.

The three enabling factors that bring Human Resource Development (HRD) to the forefront of Human Resource Management are: -

1) Acquiring or sharpening of capabilities required to perform various functions associated with their present or expected future roles.[*Acquisition* of resources]

2) Developing their general capabilities as individuals and discovering and exploiting their own inner potentials for their own or organizational purposes.[*HRD*]

3) 3.Developing organizational culture in which superior-subordinate relationship, team work and collaboration among subunits are strong and contribute to the professional well-being, motivation and pride of employees.[*Retention* of the acquired resources]

7.1. Kautilyan thought-the forerunner of Marxian Philosophy.

Apart from these three factors it has been recently proved that the conceptual application of Human Resource Development (HRD) should be in tune with the culture of the nation and its people. The great Kautilya and his conceptual analysis of HRD are to be discussed in this context; because Kautilya has worked out his concept of Human Resource Development (HRD) based on the Indian culture bed-rocked on the philosophic constituents *Dharma, Artha, Kama* and *Moksha* [*Purushartha*]. All human resource activities including the salary administration are to be placed before the principles of *Purushartha*. " The salary scale shall be such as to enable the accomplishment of state activities (by attracting the Right type of people) , shall be adequate for meeting the bodily needs of the state servants and shall not be in contradiction to the principles of *Dharma* and *Artha*" {Bk.5.Ch.3.Vs.2.}. Here the salary scale is commensurate with the accomplishment of the state-building activities and the maintenance of individual existential needs; both adhering to the principles of *Dharma, Artha, Kama* and *Moksha* [*Purushartha*]. There was in fact a strict maintenance and control of this principle and its phases of implementation; which often alleged as monarchical imposition on people. This monarchical imposition has invited sharp criticism from the Marxist schools of thinkers and ideologists. But as alleged, this monarchical interference is not an attack on the fundamental freedom of the individual or the society. This is but the powerful process of acquisition of the human asset or capital [*Prithvilabham*] and the practical process of retention of the acquired skills and knowledge [*Prithvipalanam*].

The state in Arthashastra is composed of various constituent elements which are collectively known as *Prakriti*. The state constituting these elements, *Prakriti*; is termed as *Prakriti Sampath*. *Prakriti Sampath* is the human asset or capital, which is well protected and preserved by the king. It is this human asset or capital that determines the quality of a state. *Prakriti Sampath* is composed of constituents such as: (1) the king [*Rajah* and *Yuvarajah*] (2) group of high officials [*Amathya*] (3) the territory with the inhabitants [*Janapada*] (4) the fortified towns and cities [*Durga*] (5) the treasury [*Kosa*] (6) the forces [*Dhanda*] (7) the allies [*Mitra*]. {Bk. 6.Ch.1.Vs.1.}. The higher the quality of these constituent elements [*Prakriti Sampath*], the greater will be the people's prosperity and welfare [*Yogakshema*]. If the quality of these constituent elements [*Prakriti Sampath*] is not ensured, it will weaken the people's prosperity and welfare [*Yogakshema*] and also entertain the inevitable emergence of rebels. In the 13th *Sutra* of *Chanakyasutra*, chapter 1, it is stated that the country will be ruled automatically even without a leader or a King (*Nayak or Rajah*), if the quality of these constituent elements [*Prakriti Sampath*] is ensured to bring people's prosperity and welfare [*Yogakshema*].

"Prakriti Sampatha hyanayakamapi rajyam niyathe"

Chanakyasutra-*Chapter-1*, Sutra-*13*

This epigram can be equated with the Marxian philosophy where in the final stage "the state withers away" and the people are ruled automatically even without a ruler [*Nayak*]. In Marxian philosophy, the concept of human asset or capital is treated as the proletariat; the community of the working class. It is this proletariat that in its final stage attains socialism [*Yogakshema*] and at last the state withers away. In Kautilyan context, this is a process of administrative automation with *Prithvilabham* (The acquisition of *Yogakshema* [socialist state]) and *Prithvipalanam* (The retention of the *Yogakshema* [socialist state]).

V. I. Lenin elucidates this fact:- "The first step in this process is the seizure of political power by the working class majority of society; known in Marx's day as the "dictatorship of the proletariat" as opposed to the "dictatorship of the bourgeoisie" we currently live under. Once in political power, the working class can then move to assert its control over the economy. Once the working class democratically runs the economy in the interests of all, instead of in the interests of a handful of capitalists, and then very quickly we will be able to provide the basic necessities and then much more to everyone. We will be able to abolish unemployment, provide free, quality healthcare, education, housing, and more to everyone. The creative and productive potential of humanity will be unleashed. [*Prakriti Sampath*]

As Friedrich Engels explained, this socialist "state", which would truly democratically represent the vast majority of society, would already be withering away in the proper sense of the word. The capitalist state represents a tiny minority of society, which is why they resort to such brutal measures to keep the majority under their boot. But once the state is run in the interests of the majority, then the need for police, a military, etc. will rapidly disappear along with the inequality and oppression of the capitalist system. Gradually, the coercion and compulsion of the capitalist system will disappear, replaced by the democratic administration of things in the interests of everyone [Yogakshema]". (*The State and Revolution* V. I. Lenin, 1917, www.marxists.org/archive/lenin/works/1917/staterev/ch05.htm)

Fred rich Engels

7.2. HRM and the HRM Expert-Rajahrishi.

We could see strong indications of acquisition and retention of human resources exactly in its modern form as Human resource Asset or Capital in the first chapter of the second *Adhikarana* of Arthashastra titled as *Janapadanivesam*. Here, Kautilya makes a call for the people who had left the country to return and also to prevent the existing inhabitants from leaving the country. Here Kautilya expresses his philosophy of retention of the people [human resource] the country had once retained. This is what we call as Human Resource Planning in the modern Management terminology. The basic constituents of Human Resource Management (HRM) such as Planning, Organizing, Leading and Coordinating could be seen in the *Adhikarana, Adhyakashapracharam* of Arthashastra which is calculated to have consumed a quarter share of the book. This *Adhikarana* consists of 1285 *Sutras* spread all over its 31 chapters. This *Adhikarana* describes the duties and responsibilities of 34 Heads of the Departments *(Adhyakshas). Fig: 11.* Out of which 30 Heads of Departments are from the areas related to the administrative segments such as General Administration, Defense, Industry and Trade and Commerce. The other 4 Heads of Departments are from areas related to the administrative segments such as Police Administration *(Kandakasodhanam)*, Judiciary *(Dharmastheeyam)* and Human Resource Management *(Yogavrutham)*. These heads of departments are properly controlled by the *Theerthas* we inherited from the ancient *Shastras*. They are known as *Mahamatras* in Arthashastra. "A King can reign only with the help of others, one wheel alone does not move. Therefore, a King should appoint advisers [*Mahamatras*] and listen to their advice" {Bk.1.Ch.7.Vs.9.}.

As explained in the *Sutra* above, Kautilya symbolized the system of administration as a chariot having smoothly running wheels. If one wheel among the two is not running smoothly, the chariot symbolized as the system of administration will not move forward properly. *Fig: 12.*

"Naikam chakram paribramathi"

Chanakyasutra-*Chapter-1*, Sutra-*18*

This epigrammatic presentation of Kautilya can be rightly equated with the theory of 'Organization controlling' of the modern Management. The controlling system in the modern management is an integrated control system, comprised of preliminary control, concurrent control and feedback control methods. Preliminary control is the methods that focus on the acquisition of resources. Concurrent control is the techniques and methods that focus on the actual, ongoing activity of the organization. Feedback control is the techniques and methods that analyze historical data to correct future events. If any one of the control methods (*wheel*) is not running smoothly as coordinated, the entire controlling system (*chariot*) will not move forward properly.

The amazing fact is that during B.C. 321 – B.C. 298, the great Kautilya, the father of management, had systematized the concept of Human Resource Development (HRD) based on the fundamentals of political administration and economy; adhering to the core of Indian Philosophy. The Philosophy adhered to here is the Philosophy *(Anweeshiki)* of four sciences or *Shastras*; that analyzes the impacts of *Dharma, Artha, Kama* and *Moksha* [*Purushartha*] based on the three *Vedas (Thrayi)*, Economics *(Vartha)* and the science of government *(Dhandaneethi)* so as to attain a mental state of proper equilibrium to do good to the people. The King or the ruler who is expert in all these four sciences or *Shastras* and attains the mental state of the proper equilibrium to do good to the people is known as *Rajahrishi*. Arthashastra defines, "A *Rajahrishi* [a king, wise like a sage] is one who: has self-control, having conquered the [inimical temptations] of the senses, cultivates the intellect by association of elders, keeps his eyes open through spies, is ever active in promoting the security and welfare of the people, ensures the observance [by the people] of their *Dharma* by authority and example, improves his own discipline by [continuing his] learning in all branches of knowledge and endears himself to the people by enriching them and doing good to them." {Bk.1.Ch.7.Vs.1.}.

A government headed by a *Rajahrishi,* with his self-discipline alone can guarantee security of life and welfare of the people [*Yogakshema*]. "Discipline is of two kinds – inborn and acquired. Instruction and training can promote discipline only in a person capable of benefiting from them; people incapable of [natural] self-discipline do not benefit." {Bk.1.Ch.5.Vs.1-3.}. Kautilya insists some mental faculties for the attainment of this self-discipline. They are obedience to an authoritative teacher, desire and ability to learn, capacity to retain what is learnt, understanding what is learnt, reflecting on it and finally the ability to make inferences by deliberating on the knowledge acquired. Those who are devoid of such mental faculties are not benefited by any amount of training. "A *Rajahrishi* shall always respect those councilors and *Purohitas* who warn him of the dangers of transgressing the limits of good conduct, reminding him sharply of the times prescribed for various duties and caution him even when he errs in private" {Bk.1.Ch.7.Vs.1-8.}.

This enabling of the mental faculty for acquiring the knowledge and skills through training is the core of Human Resource Development (HRD). Kautilya elucidates the idea that a trained intellect is the result of learning. Learning is attained through hearing. The trained intellect ensues by *Yoga* (successful application) and from *Yoga* comes self-possession. The final attainment of self-possession means the efficiency in acquiring knowledge. "For, a [trained] intellect is the result of learning [by hearing]; from intellect ensues [by] *Yoga* [successful application]; from *Yoga* comes self-possession. This is what meant by efficiency in acquiring knowledge." {Bk.1.Ch.5.Vs.15-16.}.

According to Kautilya civil servants should have the knowledge of the four sciences or *Shastras* such as Philosophy *(Anweeshiki)*, Three *Vedas (Thrayi)*, Economics *(Vartha)* and the science of government *(Dhandaneethi)*. *Samam, Hruku* and *Yajus* are the three *Vedas*. These *Vedas* prescribe lawful activities *(Dharma)* that help one to institute his own lawful activities *(Swadharmasthapana)* in all *Varnas* and *Ashramas*. Economics *(Vartha)* is the three-fold economic activity consists of agriculture, animal husbandry and trade and commerce. Economics *(Vartha)* contributes grains, cattle, gold, forest produce and human resources. The science of government *(Dhandaneethi)* is to check the wrong doings and to devise proper and deserving punishments to the wrongdoer so as to exercise just governance. "A king meting out unjust punishment is hated by the people he terrorizes while one who is too lenient is held in contempt; whoever imposes just and deserved punishment is respected and honoured." {Bk.1.Ch.4.Vs.7-10.}.

The *Rajahrishi* who observe the four sciences or *Shastras* should achieve ten qualities *(Sampath)* to expedite Human Resource Development. The qualities are: -(1) Leadership qualities *(Abhigamika guna)*, (2) Intellectual qualities *(Prajnanu guna)*, (3) Qualities of energy *(Utsaha guna)*, (4) Spiritual qualities *(Atma guna)*, (5) Ministral qualities *(Amatya guna)*, (6) Qualities of people *(Janapada guna)*, (7) Qualities of treasury*(Kosa guna)*, (8) Qualities of good army*(Sainya guna)*, (9) Qualities of good ally*(Mithra guna)* and (10) Favorable qualities of enemy*(Amithra guna)*. These qualities *(Sampath)* are prescribed separately to the rulers and other civil servants positioned in the hierarchy, as per their requirements; on the basis of the four sciences or *Shastra*. Fig: *13-21*.

Arthashastra is a textbook on political administration and a laboratory for economics. Hence, the book is a perfect blend of theory and experiment. It is this blend that worked for the growth and development of the administrative skills and qualities *(Sampath)* , other strategic administrative capabilities he developed through the proper application of the administrative tools he designed in the textbook and the final inferences of economics he derived in the laboratory. All these administrative skills and qualities *(Sampath)*, strategic administrative capabilities and the final inferences of economics are to be earned, experienced, developed and controlled through the art of communications, intrapersonal relationships and interpersonal relationships streamlined ultimately to control over the senses *(Indriyajaya)*.

HEADS OF DEPARTMENTS IN ARTHASHASTRA
DEFENCE MINISTRY

Sl.No.	Original Terminology	Department with details
1	Ayudhakaradhyaksha	Chief of ordinance
2	Pathyadhyaksha	Chief commander of infantry
3	Aswadhyaksha	Chief commander of cavelry
4	Hasthyadhyaksha	Chief commander of elephant corps
5	Rathadhyaksha	Chief commander of chariot corps
	FINANCE MINISTRY	
6	Kosadhyaksha	Chief superintendent of treasury
7	Koshtakaradhyaksha	Chief superintendent of warehouse
8	Akshapataladhyaksha	Chief controller of accounts and audit
	AGRICULTURE MINISTRY	
9	Seethadhyaksha	Chief superintendent of crown lands
10	Kupyadhyaksha	Chief superintendent of forest produce
11	Govadhyaksha	Chief superintendent of crown herds
12	Sunadhyaksha	Chief protector of animals and controller of animal slaughter
13	Nagavanadhyaksha	Chief elephant forester
	TRADE AND COMMERCE MINISTRY	
14	Panyadhyaksha	Chief controller of state trading
15	Samsthadhyaksha	Chief controller of private trading
16	Patanadhyaksha	Chief controller of ports and harbours

17	Sulkadhyaksha	Chief controller of customs and octroi
18	Navadhyaksha	Chief controller of shipping
19	Pouthavadhyaksha	Chief controller of weights and measures
20	Manadhyaksha	Chief surveyer and time keeper

HEADS OF DEPARTMENTS IN ARTHASHASTRA
MINISTRY OF INDUSTRY

21	Lakshanadhyaksha	Chief Master of the Mint
22	Suvarnadhyaksha	Chief superintendent of precious metals & jewellry
23	Ghanyadhyaksha	Chief superintendent of mines
24	Akaradhyaksha	Chief superintendent of mining and metallurgy
25	Lohadhyaksha	Chief superintendent of metal
26	Lavanadhyaksha	Chief Salt commissioner
27	Sutradhyaksha	Chief textile commissioner

TRANSPORT MINISTRY

28	Mudradhyaksha	Chief passport oficer
29	Vividhadhyaksha	Chief controller of pasture lands

MINISTRY OF ART AND CULTURE

30	Ganikadhyaksha	Chief controller of entertainers (Courtesans,Brothels,prostitutes and other artists)
31	Suradhyaksha	Chief controller of alchoholic beverages
32	Dhyuthadhyaksha	Chief controller of gambling

MISCELLANEOUS

33	Bandanagaradhyaksha	Chief superintendent of jail
34	Devathadhyaksha	Chief superintendent of temples

The *modus operandi* of the application of these qualities *(Sampath)* and the four sciences or *Shastras* is well explained in Arthashastra. Among these qualities; (1) Spiritual qualities, (2) Intellectual qualities, (3) Power of expressions, (4) Integrity, (5) Loyalty to the state, and (6) the Studies of four sciences or *Shastras* are the essential six basic qualities needed for the civil servants.

Kautilya has also given emphatic consideration to the vital areas of recruitment, selection, appointment, motivation and training and development; because these are the areas where the qualities *(Sampath)* and *Shastras* are to be tested and applied. Among these vital areas, the system of training and development is not found physically dominant, as it comes under education; the area, those days, was open only to the *Brahmins*. However, the ideological presence of education and training is seen imparted to the Kings, Ministers and Councilors and the same can be practicable and attainable to the people, though, not in the formal course of action but in the informal course of the sharing process.

7.3. Recruitment, Selection and Appointment in Arthashastra.

The recruitment and selection strategies of the employees in Arthashastra and their productivity and professional efficiency have greatly contributed to the proficiency and economy of the Kautilyan administration. Though it is very difficult to track the unpredictable zigzags of the bureaucrats, Kautilya has skillfully scanned even the minutest physical movement of the bureaucrats so as to check and ensure the potentials of their efficiency.

Figure: 12

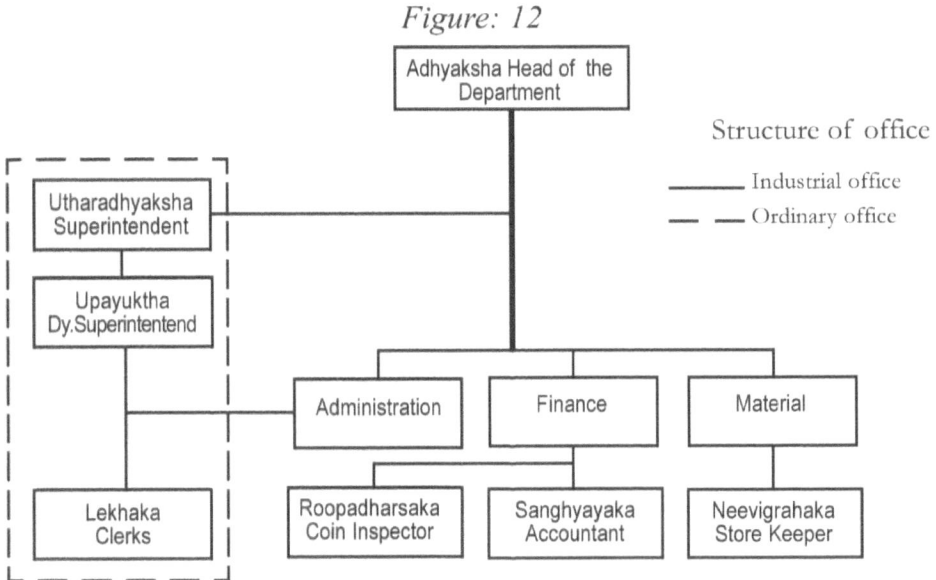

- 65 -

According to Kautilya even the soaring course of flights of birds in the sky can be predicted or fathomed; but the sly zigzag movement of the bureaucrats, targeting the illicit accumulation of public wealth cannot be predicted and fathomed. "It is possible to know even the path of birds flying in the sky but not the ways of government servants who hide their [dishonest] income." {Bk.2.Ch.9.Vs.34.}

Kautilya explains the *modus operandi* of the recruitment and selection process in the context where he discusses the appointment of the Ministers. The strategy he applied and followed in the recruitment and selection process is very much similar to that of the most modern human resource management science. In modern times there are five stages of HR process for interviewing a candidate. They are (1) The Biographical approach (2) The Criteria-based or targeted approach (3) The social accountability approach (4) The physical fitness approach (5) The emotional intelligence approach.

The Biographical approach is to gather details of qualities, nationality, family background and responsiveness to the discipline required. Kautilya verifies these qualities through a reliable person who knew the candidate well. "Of these qualities, nationality, family background and amenability to discipline shall be verified from reliable people [who know the candidate well]." {Bk.1.Ch.9.Vs.3.} The criteria-based or targeted approach is to gather details of candidate's knowledge of various skills, intelligence, perseverance, dexterity, eloquence, boldness and presence of mind. Kautilya ascertain these details from the interviewee personally. "The candidate's knowledge of the various arts shall be tested by experts in their respective fields. Intelligence, perseverance, and dexterity shall be evaluated by examining his past performance, while eloquence, boldness and presence of mind shall be ascertained by interviewing him personally." {Bk.1.Ch.9.Vs.3.} The social accountability approach is to know how far the candidate is socially accountable to the system. This is learned through watching the candidate. "Watching how he deals with others will show his energy, endurance, ability to suffer adversaries, integrity, loyalty and friendliness." {Bk.1.Ch.9.Vs.3.} The physical fitness approach is to know how physically the candidate is fit to the job. These details are gathered from the intimate friends of the candidate. "From his intimate friends, the king shall find out about his strength, health, and character (whether lazy or energetic, fickle or steady)." {Bk.1.Ch.9.Vs.3.} It is worth commendable that Arthashastra has strong references to the modern concepts of Emotional Intelligence, the modern approach is to know how far the candidate is empathic to others. The emotional intelligence is ascertained through personal observation. "The candidate's amiability and love of mankind [empathy or the absence of a tendency to hate] shall be ascertained by personal observation." {Bk.1.Ch.9.Vs.3.}

Kautilya has appointed the ministers and other civil servants only through this HR process conducted on the platform of the Indian philosophy, based on the cultural scale of *Dharma, Artha, Kama* and *Bhaya* [in this context means loyalty, honesty, uprightness and steadfastness].

Dharmopada, Arthopada, Kamopada and *Bhayopada* are the fourfold series of secret tests that resulted in the employee's refinement such as *Dharmasudhi, Arthasudhi, Kamasudhi* and *Bhayasudhi* respectively. These tests are designed to incite someone to defect by appeals to their religious sentiments or piety [*Dharmopada*], by promise of financial reward [*Arthopada*], by temptation of the flesh [*Kamopada*] or by playing on fear [*Bhayopada*]. Appointments in various departments are confirmed on the basis of these fourfold series of secret tests of refinement.

7.4. Modus Operandi of the fourfold series of secret tests.

Accordingly those who claim to have loyalty towards their country and its people are confirmed by the test, *Dharmopada* to prove *Dharmasudhi* so as to appoint them in the departments of law and justice. This "test [*Dharmopada*] is conducted by the secret agents by persuading each minister [or official], under oath of secrecy, to join a conspiracy to overthrow the King for his impiety. If any minister [or official] refuses to join, he is clean [i.e.: loyal]". {Bk.1.Ch.10.Vs.2-4.}. Those who claim that they do not sacrifice their honesty towards their country and its people for mere material gain are tested by, *Arthopada* to prove *Arthasudhi* so as to appoint them in the departments of general administration and finance administration. This "test [*Arthopada*] is conducted by the secret agents by offering bribes to various ministers [or officials], to destroy the King. If any minister [or official] refuses to bribe, he is clean [i.e.: honest]". {Bk.1.Ch.10.Vs.5-7.}. Those who claim that they do not sacrifice their uprightness towards their country and its people for mere physical pleasures are tested by the test, *Kamopada* to prove *Kamasudhi* so as to appoint them in the departments of palace and chamberlain administration. This "test [*Kamopada*] is conducted by a wandering nun by gaining the confidence of a minister [or official], in order to convey the suggestion that the queen is in love with him. Much wealth and a meeting with her shall be promised. If any minister [or official] refuses to be tempted, he is clean [i.e.: upright]". {Bk.1.Ch.10.Vs.8-10.}.Those who claim that they do not sacrifice their steadfastness towards their country and its people simply for fear of the evil and of rebel forces are tested by the test, *Bhayopada* to prove *Bhayasudhi* so as to appoint them in the departments of Defense. This "test [*Bhayopada*] is conducted by a minister who shall invite; all other ministers [or officials] for a party. Seemingly apprehending the conspiracy, the King shall throw them all in jail. An intelligence officer, previously placed for in the same jail, shall try to induce them to kill the King who had deprived them of their honours and prosperity. If anyone [minister or official] refuses to be induced, he is clean [i.e.: steadfast]" {Bk.1.Ch.10.Vs.11-12.}.

In order to maintain the integrity and honesty of the tests; the King, the queen and other supreme officers are not allowed to interfere in these tests. Because Kautilya does not believe in any sort of remedial measures; by which the above-mentioned disqualifications can be transformed to qualifications. If any deliberate attempts were made to qualify the disqualified, it would be like adding poison to water. "Under no circumstances shall the King make himself or his [principal] queen the target for ascertaining the probity of a minister. Furthermore, he shall not corrupt the uncorrupted; that would be like adding poison to water; for, it may well happen that a cure may not be found for one so corrupted. Even the mind of the steadfast and the valiant may not return to its original purity if it is perverted by the fourfold secret test. Hence, the King shall make an outsider the object of reference for the tests and then keep the ministers under surveillance using clandestine agents" {Bk.1.Ch.10.Vs.17-20.}.

7.5. Modus Operandi *of Interview and Performance appraisal.*

It is indeed a remarkable observation on the diplomacy in Arthashastra, that the ministers are appointed and made permanent only after successfully getting through the said fourfold series of secret tests, to prove their cultural and diplomatic cleanliness, as explained above. There is also a sound reference to the procedure of an interview conducted by the king for the aspirant who seeks the king's service [civil service]. "After obtaining an audience with a good king, the aspirant shall discuss [political] science with him. [The reason being:] His position will be secure only when the ruler holds opinions which are not contrary to [the teachings of] political science. If the king asks questions which require intelligent consideration, the aspirant shall reply briefly, [strictly] in accordance with the eternal principles of *Dharma* and *Artha*, without being afraid of those present." {Bk.5.Ch.4.Vs.4-6.}. It is also a noticeable fact that those who have failed in these tests and interview are to be placed somewhere in the isolated mines or forests where no direct public interaction or conduct with people are possible.

After qualifying the fourfold series of secret tests, there is an effective monitoring mechanism to observe and evaluate the behaviour, professional efficiency and productivity of ministers or officials [employees] appointed. This monitoring mechanism the equivalent of Performance Appraisal shows how far advanced the behavioral science and the personality development were in those days. "[The appointee] shall always be at the side of the king [or officer], neither too close nor too far away; not talk slyly against other advisers [or officers]; not say things which are not carefully thought out and which are untrue, uncultured, or outside his knowledge; not laugh loudly when there is nothing to laugh about; when there is cause, he may laugh but not loudly; avoid [uncouth behaviour like] spitting and breaking wind; neither talk in secret with another [adviser or officer] nor become quarrelsome in public debate [or meeting]; not dress [above his station or class] like royalty nor in a gaudy or clownish fashion; not openly ask for gems or special favours [tips]; not indulge in [unseemly gestures like] winking, biting lips and frowning; not interrupt while another speaking; not antagonize the powerful; and not associate with [disreputable] women, pimps, envoys, of neighbouring kings, those supporting the enemy, dismissed officers, wicked people, those who form a group for a single objective nor with specialized lobbies.". {Bk.5.Ch.4.Vs.8-10, 14.}.

Figure: 13

IMPORTANT QUALITIES FOR THE MINISTERS
AMATHYA GUNAS

Sl.No.	Qualities for the ministers
1	Be a natural citizen or Janapadan
2	Have noble birth
3	Be agreeable to the people
4	Be proficient in all kinds of Arts
5	Have an eye of science and awareness of science
6	Be intellectual
7	Be hard working
8	Be cleaver and skillful
9	Be wise and less takative
10	Be brave
11	Have creative energy
12	Be energetic
13	Be powerfull with reason
14	Be tolerant
15	Have Dharmic cleanliness
16	Have an ally attitude
17	Be stable and dedicative
18	Have good character and habits
19	Have physical health and spiritual power
20	Have the spirit of deliverance and free from selfishness
21	Be dynamic in all activitie

Figure: 14

IMPORTANT LEADERSHIP QUALITIES
ABHIGAMIKA GUNAS

Sl.No.	Leadership Qualities
1	Born in high or noble family
2	Endowed with good fortune, intelligence and spirit
3	Guided and enlightened by elders
4	Be pious
5	Always speak truth
6	Not to break promises
7	Be grateful
8	Be liberal
9	Be energetic
10	Not to be a delayed decision maker
11	Endowed with controllable neighbouring princes
12	Be resolute
13	Have a healthy cabinet
14	Desirous to be traine

Figure: 15

IMPORTANT QUALITIES FOR A RULER

SWAMI GUNAS

Sl.No.	Original Terminology	Translated terminology
1	Abhigamika guna	Leadership qualities
2	Prajnanu guna	Intellectual qualities
3	Utsaha guna	Qualities of energy
4	Atma guna	Spiritual qualities
5	Janapada guna	Qualities of people
6	Kosa guna	Qualities of treasury
7	Sainya guna	Qualities of arm

Figure: 16

IMPORTANT INTELLECTUAL QUALITIES

PRAJNANU GUNAS

Sl.No.	Intellectual Qualities
1	Desire to listen and learn
2	Patience to listen
3	Ability to grasp
4	Ability for thorough understanding
5	Ability to reflect knowledge
6	Power of speculation and reasoning
7	Urge for absolute trut

Figure:17

IMPORTANT SPIRITUAL QUALITIES
ATMA GUNAS

Sl.No.	Spiritual Qualities
1	Qualities of personal excellence
2	Be bold
3	Have memory, intellect and strength
4	Be exalted
5	Have managerial capacity
6	Be trained in Arts
7	Be free from vices
8	Able to lead the Army
9	Ability to oblige and revenge properly, observing Dharma
10	Have sense of shame
11	Ability to utilize resources during the times of crisis and normality
12	Have long vision or far-sightedness
13	Be conscious of place, time and human resources
14	Ability to know treaties and rivalries
15	Have know-how of give and take economic policy
16	Know the weak points of others
17	Be well guarded
18	Not to laugh at others
19	Look straight with consideration
20	Devoid of Lust, Anger, Greed, Stubbornness, Fickleness and Misery
21	Speak pleasantly and sweetly
22	Speak positively with a smile
23	Accept the advice of the elders and obey the traditions

Figure:18

IMPORTANT QUALITIES OF PEOPLE
JANAPADA GUNAS

Sl.No.	Qualities of people
1	Have forts in the middle and frontiers
2	Have rich Granery during crisis of famine
3	Have complete safety and security
4	Safeguard livilihood
5	Have power enough to defend the enemy
6	Have weak neighbouring princes
7	Have comfortable and safe land
8	Have rich agriclture land, mines and forests
9	Capacitated for HRD
10	Have rich pastures, animals and water resources
11	Facilitated with full of land and water routes
12	Availability of consumer goods
13	Enriched revenue through dhanda and taxes
14	Have a potential farming community
15	Have wise and rich people
16	Have good population of Sudras or lower varnas
17	Have full of patriotic, faithfull and submissive people

IMPORTANT QUALITIES OF ENERGY
UTSAHA GUNAS

Sl.No.	Qualities of energy
1	Bravery
2	Resentment
3	Quickness
4	Dexterit

Figure: 20
IMPORTANT QUALITIES OF TREASURY
KOSA GUNAS

Sl.No.	Qualities of Treasury
1	Have own savings and inherited savings as per Dharma or righteousness
2	Have rich treasure of gold and silver
3	Have rich treasure of gems and gold coins
4	Powerfull enough to overcome calamitie

Figure: 21
IMPORTANT QUALITIES OF ARMY
SAINYA GUNAS

Sl.No.	Qualities of Army
1	Have inherited paternal power
2	Have constant, covetable and prosperous Army
3	Never to be frustrated
4	Have tolerance
5	Have rich experience in wars
6	Fully trained in all warfare
7	Able to share the bad times of the king and abstain from spirit of disintegration
8	Richly inhabited by the Kshatriya

This monitoring mechanism is operated through the department of espionage or vigilance. This department consists of two monitoring squads known as (1) the stationary squad i.e. secret agents based in one place *(Samstham)*, consisting of the intelligence officer (*Kapatika*), spies under the cover of monks (*Udhasthitha*), householders (*Grihapatikavyajna*), merchants (*Vydhehakavyajna*) and ascetics (*Thapasavyajna*); and (2) the mobile squad i.e. the roving secret agents *(Sancharam)*, consists of the secret agent (*Sathrin*), the assassin (*Theekshna*), the poisoner (*Rasadha*) and the women mendicant (*Bhikshuki*). These squads are to find out the presence of the knowledge of the four sciences or *Shastra* in the required proportion among the officials and also to check whether the sciences are applied properly in their professions or not. *Fig: 22.*

7.6. Administrative Paternalism and Management.

The administrative system in Arthashastra is not the invention of a single genius. It is but the result of an evolution of the social and politicaldevelopment through the *Shastras* or Classics or *Ithihasas* of the *Vedic* period. Its aim is to establish the theory of acquisition (*Prithvilabham*) and retention (*Prithvipalanam*) of resources to attain the welfare and prosperity of the people *(Yogakshema)* in all its diversities.

We could observe a kind of extreme administrative paternalism which regulated the relationship among classes to minimize the social distance and utilized their resources for the attainment of welfare and prosperity of the people *(Yogakshema)*. The four key factors of the administrative paternalism are ***controlling*** the civil servants [and the people as a whole] and prevent them from making money through unauthorized or fraudulent ways; ***motivating*** the civil servants [and the people as a whole] for their good service; ***organizing*** the civil servants [and the people as a whole] to collect the proper revenue from people in time; and finally ***leading*** the civil servants [and the people as a whole] towards the architecture of an ideal state. The King will make regular and timely inspection of the civil service and the public life for the observance of his paternalistic duties and responsibilities. "The King shall have the work of the Heads of departments inspected daily, for men are, by nature, fickle and, like horses, change after being put to work. Therefore, the King shall acquaint himself with all the details [of each departments or undertakings, such as] – the officer responsible, the nature of work, the place of work, the time taken to do it, the exact work to be done, the outlay and the profit" [Bk.2.Ch.9.Vs.2, 4.].

This administrative paternalism is very much evident in times of political crisis and natural calamities where people want more favours and allowances from the king. "Whenever danger threatens, the King shall protect all those afflicted like a father [protects his children] and shall organize continuous [day and night] prayers with oblations" [Bk.4.Ch.3.Vs.42, 43.]. "He shall, however, treat leniently, like a father [would treat his son], those, whose exemptions have ceased to be effective" {Bk.2.Ch.1.Vs.18}. It is the expression of pure paternal care and of absolute exposition of an administrative culture that is far beyond a mere political exercise. It targets the realization of the prosperity of the people and the state [*Yogakshema*]. In Arthashastra we could see the identified interests of the governance and the governed. We could see there, the envious blend of national resources of wealth and rational human resources that bring wealth and welfare. This perfect blend of economics and human resources leads to state socialism that focuses on social solidarity and social happiness; attained through the system of equal distribution of resources of wealth, welfare, individual concern and the strict control over production and the totality of the enforced discipline in the state. This equality in distribution of resources and welfare in Arthashastra has been criticized in all times, on the ground that the twice-born higher *Varna* people have enjoyed unequal or excess privileges. This disagreement with the equality is because of the characteristic socialistic pattern of India, where social equality never becomes a political equality. However, this spirit of equality in Arthashastra is seen to have been excessively exercised and extended to the uncompromising maintenance of the law and social order, economic stability, sustenance of the livelihood, prevention of suffering among people, consumer protection and even the welfare of the slaves and prisoners.

7.7. Dasatwa-*the glowing light of liberalism.*

The term slaves and bonded labour in Arthashastra are *Dasa* or *Ahitaka* which simply means servants who enjoyed fewer rights than other employees, and depended upon employers for ensuring their individual and family existence. It is more significant than that of a system of bonded labour. It is not exactly the slave as in the ancient Greece or in the modern Africa. Kautilya, in fact, uses a variety of other expressions such as *Dasa* (bonded labourer/slave), *Dasatwa* (concept of bonded labour/slavery), *Dasabhava* (State of being a bonded labourer/slave) and *Dasakalpa* (Rules regarding bonded labourer/slave), *Udaradasatwa* (bonded labour for maintenance), *Ahithaka* (bonded labour under mortgage), *Karmakara* (bonded casual labourers), *Bruthaka* (bonded contract labourers), *Gramabruthaka* (bonded labourers with handcraft); to denote different aspects of this phenomenon. These expressions convey the fact that Kautilya might have preserved a community of *Dasas* for the service of the twice born higher *Varnas* just like the *Devadasi* system. Because as Kautilya mentions; there were free and unfree status to persons [probably *Dasas*] during his period and nobody is allowed to change the status [free or bonded] by any force. "Changing by force the free or unfree status of a person is a serious offence punishable with a fine of 1000 *Panas*" {Bk.3.Ch.20.Vs.19.}. This also implies the fact that the King is the ultimate power that controlled the course of life of the *Dasas* rather than their masters. "The King shall enforce the laws regarding the slaves and bonded labour" {Bk.2.Ch.1.Vs.25.}. To some extent Kautilya implies that even an *Arya* could be a slave. "Anyone who fails to set free a slave on receipt of redemption money shall not only be fined but the culprit shall be kept in detention until the slave is freed" {Bk.3Ch.13.Vs.21.}. Kautilya has also framed some rules to protect these *Dasas* or servants. "The regulations about bonded labour apply to anyone (i) who mortgages himself; (ii) is mortgaged by someone else; (iii) is sent, in times of distress, to work for someone in return for maintenance (*Udaradasa*); (iv) works off a fine or (v) is captured in war" {Bk.3Ch.13.Vs.16,18, 19.}.

Figure: 22

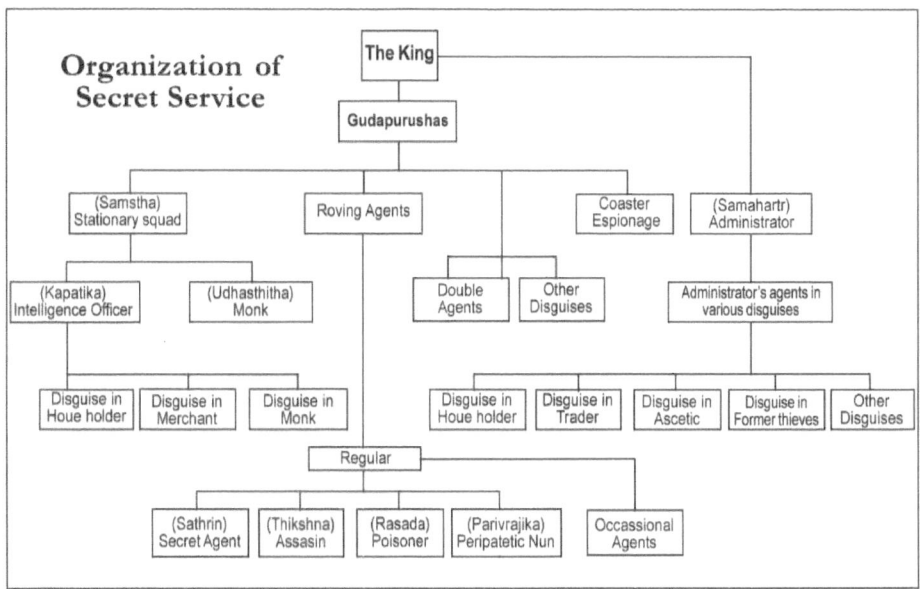

After citing the records of *Magasthenes* that 'all Indians are free and not one of them is a slave'; R.K. Mookerjee establishes the fact that the supposed slavery in India was of such mild character [*Dasabhava*] and limited extent [*Udaradasa*] as compared withthe slavery known to the Hellenic world, *Magesthenes,* could notnotice its existence. Here the bondage with the labourer is valuedand justifiably compensated with other resources, after evaluatingthe value of the labour output. V.I. Kalyanov, the Russian commentator has placed the text in the period of transition betweenthe decay of the slave owning society and the rise of early feudalism. In brief, it can be concluded that Kautilya's attitude towards slavery stands apart as a glowing light of liberalism and humanity in a barbaric age.

7.8. Administration: The structure and Philosophy.

The basic units of Arthashastra mode of administration are its villages. Villages in Arthashastra are cooperative social units managed by *Gramikas* [Village heads] advised by *Gramavrudhas* [Village elders]. The general administration of the state as a whole is managed by such small cooperative social units of grouped villages and its offices of administration. Accordingly *Samgrahana* is constituted of a group of ten villages, *Kharvatika* of two hundred villages, *Dhronamukha* of four hundred villages and *Sthaneeya* of eight hundred villages. *Janapa-*

da is constituted of four *Sthaneeya* or three thousand and two hundred villages. Each *Janapada* consists of five *mandalas* or circle such as ally *(Mitra)*, enemy *(Ari/Amitra)*, conqueror *(Vijigishu)*, the middle King *(Madhyama)* and the neutral King *(Udhaseena)*. These *Janapadas* have multiplied themselves and developed to form states and confederation of states or *Rashtra*. But Kautilya called them either *Janapada* or *Prithvi* as a part of his affinity towards the land and culture rather brand them as a political establishment *(Chakravarti Mandala)*. *Fig: 23.*

Figure: 23

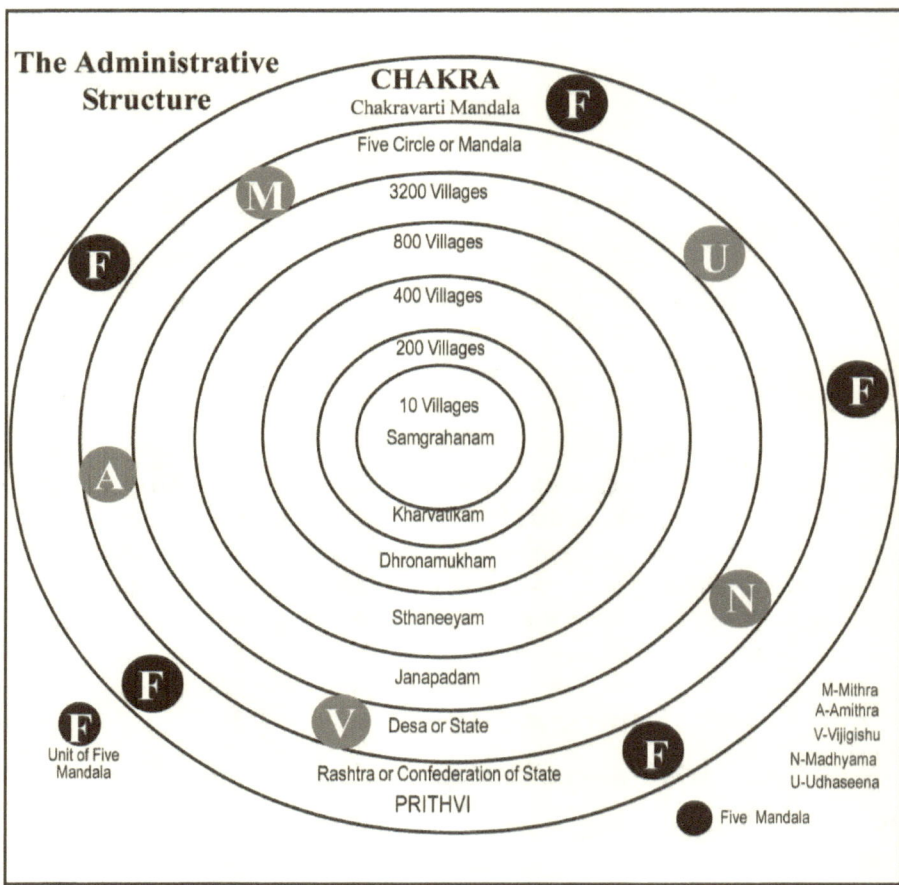

The theory of five *Mandalas* or the circle of the states and its foreign policy works on focusing a particular King, from whose point of view the internal situation of the state is analyzed. Kautilya designated this King as *Vijigishu* – the King who wants to win or the would-be-conqueror. A neighbouring King is then designated as the enemy (*Ari*) and other King nearby as allies (*Ally*), a middle King (*Madhyama*) or neutral (*Udhaseena*) King. The terminology defines only a set of relationships (*Mandala*). This needs to be emphasized because the conqueror is not necessarily a good King and correspondingly, the enemy a bad King. The advice given to the conqueror can equally be applied by the enemy. Among these *mandalas,* the *mandalas* of ally King (*Ally*) and enemy King (*Ari*) consist of five constituents each and the *mandalas* of middle King and neutral King consists of single constituents each to form twelve Kingly constituents (*Rajaprakritis*). Each of these Kingly constituents consist of five other constituents known as ministers or councilors (*Amatyar*), country side (*Janapada*), fortified cities (*Dhurga*), treasury (*Kosa*) and army (*Dhanda*) to form sixty material constituents (*Dhravyaprakritis*). The synergy of these twelve Kingly constituents (*Rajaprakritis*) and sixty material constituents (*Dhravyaprakritis*) totaled to seventy two *Prakritis,* determines the power of the King in Arthashastra. This synergy of power has been beautifully symbolized as a wheel, positioning him [the king] at the hub and the allies drawn to him by the spokes of the wheel separated by inter-

Figure: 24

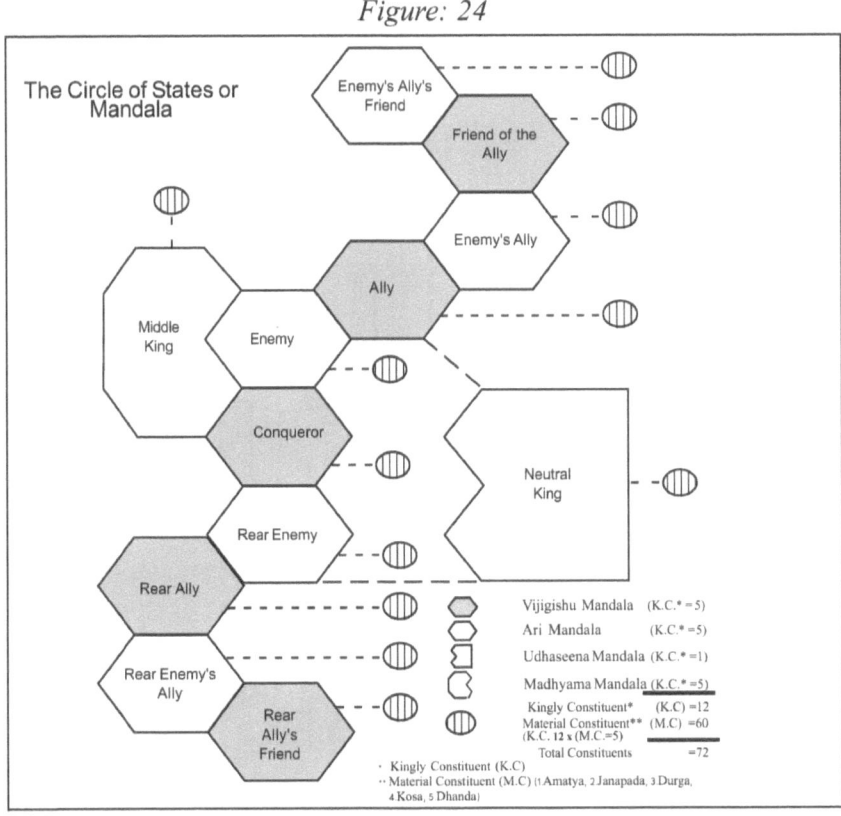

Figure: 25

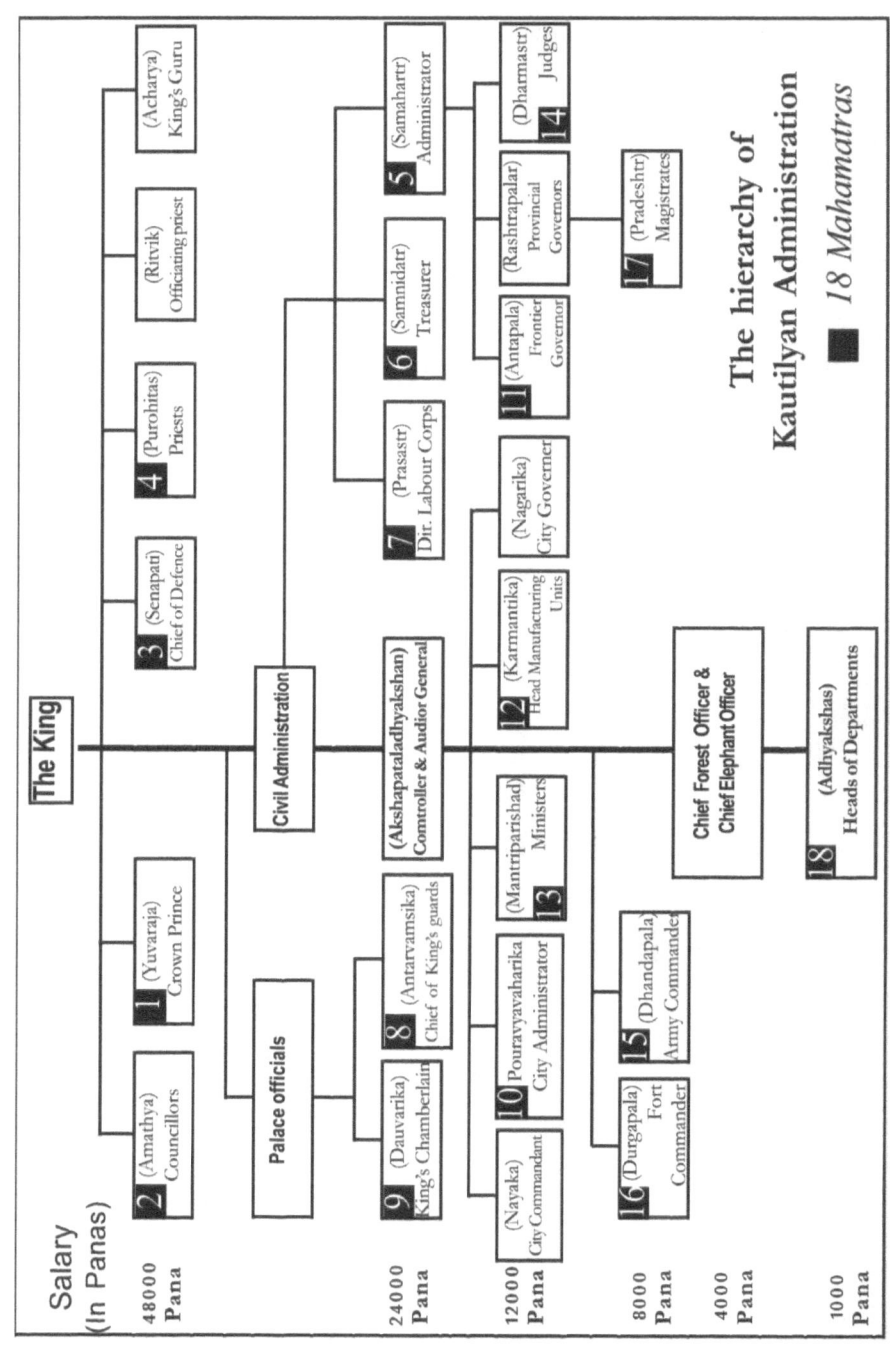

The hierarchy of Kautilyan Administration

■ *18 Mahamatras*

vening territory as its rim. "The conqueror shall think of the circle of the states as a wheel – himself at the hub and his allies, drawn to him by the spokes though separated by intervening territory, as its rim" {Bk.6.Ch.2.Vs.39.}. *Fig: 24.*

The Kautilyan state displays a miniature of its kind or a cross section of the welfare state fully realized by the great Kautilya. The span of administration and the strategy of the foreign policy theorized by Kautilya are limited to the Indian subcontinent. As per historical records, the Kautilyan state where the theories of Arthashastra were practiced, has an area of 15, 000, 00 Square Kilometers with three crores of population. "The area extending from Himalayas in the north to the sea in the south and a thousand *Yojanas* wide from east to west is the area of opera- tion of the King emperor" {Bk.9.Ch.1.Vs.17,18.}. Territories beyond this area are not included, probably for the reason that the conqueror is not intended to establish a social order based on the *Arya's Dharma, Varna* and *Ashrama* system in the conquered territories forcibly but subject to the practicality and desirability of its people. *Fig: 2.*

The Kautilyan state is steered by eighteen categories of *Mahamatras* (high officials) posi- tioned at the helm of the administration. "The king shall select, from among the roving spies, those who are diligent, can disguise themselves credibly conforming to different regions, and who know various languages and professions to spy on the activities of the [eighteen ranks of] high officials within the country. They shall serve the king with devotion and to the best of their ability." {Bk.1.Ch.12.Vs.6.} This hierarchical order is indebted to the hierarchy of eighteen *Theerthas* during the *Smritis* periods. R.P. Kangle identified exactly eighteen *Mahamatras* num- bered as: 1. Crown Prince *(Yuvaraja)* 2. Minister *(Amathya)* 3. Commander-in-chief *(Senapati)* 4. Chaplain *(Purohita)* 5. Administrator *(Samahartr)* 6. Director of stores/treasurer *(Samnidhatr)* 7. Director Labour Corps *(Prasastr)* 8. Chief of Palace Guards *(Antarvamsika)* 9. Chief Palace Usher *(Dauvarika)* 10. Commandant *(Pauravyavaharika)* 11. Commander of the Frontier Forts *(Antapala)* 12. Director of Factories *(Karmantika)* 13. The Council of Ministers *(Mantriparishad)* 14. City judge *(Dharmastr?)* 15. Chief of Army Staff *(Dhandapala)* 16. Commander of Fort *(Durgapala)* 17. Magistrate *(Pradestr)* 18. Superintendent *(Adhyaksha)*. The duties and responsibilities of these *Mahamatras* in general are: to maintain a perfect law and order situation in the society; to protect the personal life and property; to help all people above caste or creed for the attainment of their material welfare; to safeguard all people from all crisis of life, above their caste or creed; to ensure a strong base of industrial and cultural growth; to ensure social solidarity; to provide all sorts of relief to the farmers and to compensate the *Sudras* who have worked in the land of *Vaishya* for a period of five years. [The germination of "Sons of Soil revolution"] *Fig: 25.*

In the administrative hierarchy constituted by the *Mahamatras, Samahartr* (Administrator) is considered to have a dominant and dynamic role in the administration. When compared to the modern administrative hierarchy, the role of *Samahartr* (Administrator) can be equated with the role of the Chief Finance Secretary. The main duties of *Samahartr* are revenue collection, maintenance of law and order of the whole country side and also in charge of the secret services. (Department of intelligence or vigilance) "The *Samahartr* (Administrator) shall be responsible for: (a) the collection of revenue from the fortified towns, the countryside, the mines, the irrigation works, forests and trade routes (b) the preparation of the budget and maintenance of detailed accounts of revenue and expenditure as prescribed. A wise administrator is one who collects revenue so as (c) to increase income and reduce expenditure. He shall (d) take remedial measures if income diminishes and expenditure increases." {Bk.2.Ch.6.Vs.1, 10-28.}.

Samahartr (Administrator) has absolute control over the country except the areas of the fortified cities. It is he who has the right to appoint the *Sthanikas* (District Administrators) who are in charge of each *Sthaneeyas* (Districts). Though the Head Quarters of *Samahartr* (Administrator) is the capital city, he will be always stationed in the villages and worked with the *Gopan* (Thahasildar) who is in charge of *Samgrahanas* (Revenue Zone) which consists of eight or ten villages. The most important feature of *Samahartr's* (Administrator) administration is that they governed the country in accordance with the advices of the *Gramavrudhas* (Village Elders). Unlike the modern administration, Arthashastra administration has preserved the cultural sanctity and heritage of the villages and provided maximum welfare, safety and security to the villagers. Hence, the *Samahartr* is always vigilant on the undesirable persons or forces that are adversely acting upon the normal village life and such forces are eliminated timely. "There are thirteen types of undesirable persons who amass wealth secretly by causing injury to the population. [These undesirable persons [forces] are: (1) Corrupt Judges (2) Corrupt Magistrates (3) Corrupt Heads of villages (4). Departments that extorts money from the public (5) Perjurers (6) Procurers of perjury (7) Witchcraft men (8) Black magic men (9) Sorcerers (10) Poisoners (11) Narcotic dealers (12) Counterfeiters (13) Adulterers of precious metals.] When they are exposed by secret agents, they shall either be exiled or made to pay adequate compensation proportionate to the gravity of the offence." {Bk.4.Ch.4.Vs.23.}

Samnidhatr (Director of stores/Treasurer) is the second dominant high level officer in the administrative hierarchy. R.P. Kangle translates *Samnidhatr* as the Director of stores. But the scholars like R.K. Mookerji and L.N. Rangarajan translates him as Treasurer. Since the *Artha* concept in Arthashastra involves money and other material resources, Kangle's translation is more apt and justifiable. "The *Samnidhatr* (Director of stores/Treasurer) shall be responsible for the construction of all buildings concerned with storing government property, namely, the treasury, the commodity warehouse, the granary, the store for forest produce and the ordinance depots. He shall be responsible for the construction of jails." {Bk.2.Ch.5.Vs.1.}. *Samnidhatr* (Director of stores/Treasurer) is the barometer of the income-expenditure-net balance level of the country. He is the main determinant of the profit making mechanism of the country. His role is that of a financial analyst. "He shall have so thorough a knowledge of the receipts and disbursements from the city and from the countryside that, when questioned, he shall not falter in giving details of the income, expenditure and net balance for [accounts relating to] a period of even a hundred years." {Bk.2.Ch.5.Vs.22.}. "If the treasurer [Director of stores] causes loss to the treasury due to ignorance he shall be censured and if it is deliberate he shall be whipped; those abetting him shall receive half the punishment." {Bk.2.Ch.5.Vs.16-19.}.

In all the stages of growth and development of the country i.e. from the lowest administrative segment, *Samgrahana* to the highest administrative system, *Prithvi*; the dominant forces of agriculture and agro-economics are vibrantly present. Fig: 19. The human resources behind these dominant forces are *Sudras* and *Kshudrakas*; the dynamic grassroots which accelerated agriculture and agro-economics. This is the one major reason for keeping away the *Vaishyas, Kshathriyas* and the *Brahmins* from the villages. In fact, the *Vaishyas, Kshathriyas* and the *Brahmins* have their own social responsibilities to be fulfilled and realized in their own *Dharmic* circles or *Ashramas* for begetting benefits and perfecting the social system. "It is preferable to induct the [three] lower *Varnas* [practicing the three main areas of economic activity] because of the variety of benefits which flow from them. Farmers are dependable and productive; cowherds make agriculture and other activities possible [by opening up pasture lands]; and rich traders are a source of goods and loans [of money]." {Bk.7.Ch.11.Vs.20-21}.This is the social science of disengagement and detachment of the *Varnas* from each other for the corporate gain of the ultimate performance of the society. This state of disengagement and intentional detachment of the higher caste from the lower castes in the villages might have been later exploited by the higher caste, *Brahmins*; to bring in the diverse spirit of discrimination and the evil of social marginalization among the castes.

This social science of disengagement and detachment of the *Varnas* from each other has acted as an objective correlative for the physical development of the country's treasury, money, grain, food drinks and psychological development of the human resources; that have transported the country to welfare and prosperity. It is this specific role-play among the higher *Varnas* that denied the lower *Varnas*, the right to education and learning. Here the denial of the right to education and learning to the lower *Varnas* is not a denial on the ground of discrimination but an indispensable factor to integrate the social economics of Kautilya. So it is better to understand and support the idea of the integrated social development of Kautilya rather than allege him to be the denier of rights and privileges to the lower *Varnas*.

The concept of *Artha* in Arthashastra needs serious social research to find out its real core. A majority of researchers so far, has limited the concept of *Artha* to the synonym of money. But *Artha* according to Kautilya has the implied meanings such as land, money, grain, gold and the implication even grows and develops to the greater extend of human resources or labour *(Vishti)*. Human resource is the labour force. In other words, Labour force attributes to money. Hence, human resource in Arthashastra is accounted for, in terms of money and also treated as both revenue and expenditure. In the areas of taxes and penalty, the value of human resource is made equivalent to the value of tax and penalty. It means that, in Arthashastra, tax or penalty can be paid as human resources. Accordingly human resources have become a vital head of revenue and expenditure in the balance sheet and profit and loss accounts in Arthashastra. This decisive and monetary role of human resource in the accounting concept of Arthashastra proves that our innovative concept of Human Resource Accounting is not at all as innovative as we claim now, but only a continuation of the accounting concepts already triggered in Arthashastra.

It is remarkably surprising to find that Kautilya has given indomitable importance to the human resource factor in the overall administration of the state. The key elements of Human Resource Management System such as planning, organizing, leading, controlling, and the feedback process are thoroughly discussed and displayed in Arthashastra. The five aspects of Human Resource Management System cited are; "the objectives to be achieved [planning], the availability of men and materials [Organizing], the means of carrying out the task [leading], deciding on the time and place of action [Controlling] and contingency plans against failure [feedback]". {Bk.1.Ch.15.Vs.42.}. Rightly observing the five elements of the Human Resource Management System, Kautilya designs the proper course of action and implements the project promptly. "Deliberations shall not be unduly delayed once an opportunity for action arises. No one, who belongs to the side likely to be adversely affected by the project, shall be consulted." {Bk.1.Ch.15.Vs.45-46}.

According to Kautilya's Philosophy of HRD, there are six senses or enemies *(Arishadwarghas)* within a person to be either renounced or controlled. The balanced renunciation of the six senses or enemies *(Arishadwarghas)* brings total control over senses *(Indriyajaya)*. The six senses to be renounced or controlled are the lust *(Kama)*, anger *(Krodh)*, greed *(Lobh)*, conceit *(Mana)*, arrogance *(Madha)*, and foolhardiness *(Harsha)*. These are basically derived from the over-indulgence of *Panchendriya* [five senses of hearing, touch, sight, taste and smell]. "Self-control, which is the basis of knowledge and discipline, is acquired by giving up lust [*Kama*], anger [*Krodh*], greed [*Lobh*], conceit [*Mana*], arrogance [*Madha*], and foolhardiness [*Harsha*]. Living in accordance with the *Shastras* means avoiding over-indulgence in all pleasures of [the senses i.e.] hearing, touch, sight, taste and smell." {Bk.1.Ch.6.Vs.1-2.}. There is a strong reference to the six senses and enemies *(Arishadwarghas)* to be renounced in the *Sri Chanakya Niti-Sastra; The Political Ethics Of Chanakya Pandit* (Raja Ram Kumar Press, Lucknow, 1981) translated and edited by Miles Davis. "If you wish to gain control of the world by the performance of a single deed, then keep the following fifteen, which are prone to wander here and there, from getting the upper hand of you: the five sense objects (objects of sight, sound, smell, taste, and touch); the five sense organs (ears, eyes, nose, tongue and skin) and organs of activity (hands, legs, mouth, genitals and anus)". {Ch.14.13}.

This control over senses *(Indriyajaya)* helps the person to observe the four sciences or *Shastra (Anweeshiki, Thrayi, Vartha* and *Dhandaneethi)* and to acquire the capabilities that are required for the Human Resource Development. It is these controls that prevent the King, ministers and other officers from self-destructions. *Sri Chanakya Niti-Sastra; The Political Ethics Of Chanakya Pandit* (Raja Ram Kumar Press, Lucknow, 1981) translated and edited by Miles Davis has referred to this: "Excessive attachment to sense pleasures leads to bondage, and detachment from sense pleasures leads to liberation; therefore it is the mind alone that is responsible for bondage or liberation." {Ch.13.12}

At the same time Kautilya reminds us to keep up the equilibrium of the five senses *(Panchendriya)* and to preserve the physical potential of the individual along with the control over six senses or enemies *(Arishadwarghas)*. "There is no need for such a king to deprive himself of all sensual pleasures [and lead a life of total austerity] so long as he does not infringe his *Dharma* or harms his own material well-being." {Bk.1.Ch.7.Vs.4.}.

The administration methodology in Arthashastra has mainly three approaches. They are (i) direct approach, (ii) indirect approach and (iii) inferential approach. The direct approach is a first-hand approach steered by the monarch, the King. The indirect approach is a second hand approach operated through the skillful movement of the espionage or vigilance department. The inferential approach is the presumptive approach to find the undone action from the actions done. The decision making and foreseeing capacity of the King is seen in the inferential approach. But the critics of Arthashastra have observed and alleged the presence of a militant approach in the Kautilyan administration. This is only a superficial perspective. Because on closer examination one could see the allegation baseless and feel the presence of the most effective conciliatory approach, the modern Human Resource Management tool.

7.9. Conflict Management in Arthashastra.

Kautilya has opened a wide discussion on the conflict management and devised effective solutions for solving the conflicts in Arthashastra. Conflicts are emerged due to various discontents among people. The causes of discontents are classified as four types. They are anger *(Krodh)*, fear *(Bheethi)*, greed *(Lobh)* and conceit *(Mana)*. Hence, there are discontented people of anger (*Krudhavargha*), discontented people of fear *(Bheethivargha)*, discontented people of greed *(Lubdhavargha)* and the discontented people of conceit *(Manivargha)*. These people, for the cause they belong to, will be gradually instigated and join with the external forces to form a rebel group. This group then becomes a threat to the country. Hence, they should be attended to and managed well to safeguard the integrity of the country. "The discontented persons shall not be allowed to come together and join hands with neighboring princes, jungle chiefs, kinsmen who covet throne and disgruntled princes; sowing dissension [*Bhedham*] is the method to be used" {Bk.1.Ch.13.Vs.17-21.}. Fig: 26.

The HRD strategies applied for confronting these discontented people are conciliation *(Samam)*, placating with rewards and gifts *(Upapradhanam)*, sowing dissension among enemies

(Bhedham) and enforcement *(Dhanda)*. These strategies are applied in the natural order *(Anuloma)* and unnatural order *(Prathiloma)* according to the gravity of the discontent. "The methods can be used singly or in combination depending on the seriousness of the situation. There are four ways of using any one method, six ways of using two at a time, four ways of using three at a time and one way of using the methods singly or in any of the possible combinations in the *Anuloma* [natural] order. Likewise, there are fifteen ways of using them in the *Prathiloma* [unnatural] order. If only one method is recommended, it is defined as 'placing a restriction', if a choice is suggested, it is an 'option' and if two or more are to be used together, it is a 'combination'." {Bk.9.Ch.7.Vs.73-79}. The strategy of conciliation *(Samam)* consists of six ways to confront the problem. They are praising the merits, mutual human relations, mutual sharing of benefits, inducement of hopes, identity of interest and mutual awarding and honoring. The strategy of conciliation *(Samam)* approach; acts as a Grievance Handling Machinery especially with its way of 'inducement of hopes'. The aggrieved servant is given a chance for rethinking and purgation and to clear out the misunderstanding between him and the king [or the officer]. "[When he leaves the king's service,] the courtier [servant] may seek the intervention of a close friend of the monarch [acts as a Grievance Handling Officer]. He shall stay with the friend and, through him and other friends try to remove the [king's] misunderstanding about him. If he succeeds, he can return to his position." {Bk.5.Ch.5.Vs.12-14}.The strategy of placating with rewards and gifts *(Upapradhanam)* consists of five ways of approaching the problems. They are relinquishing what is owed, continuing a payment already being made, returning of something received, giving something new out of one's own wealth, and permission to take something from the enemy. The only way to confront the problems through sowing dissension among enemies *(Bhedham)* is the divide and rule strategy. It can be inferred that during the pre-independent period of India, the British imperialists have applied this strategy to sabotage the unity and integrity of Indians. These strategies of conflict management can be used either in the natural order *(Anuloma)* or unnatural order *(Prathiloma)* applying reason or intelligence. The fourth strategy, enforcement *(Dhanda)* can only be applied if the other three strategies fail in the course of solving the conflicts. Fig: 26.

7.10. Empowering and Regulating Administrative system.

Arthashastra deals with so many subjects connected with political diplomacy and administration. The craftsmanship of Kautilya in organizing the subjects has made the work sublime. The reason for the success with the craftsmanship and sublimity is the undercurrent of the practical economy that Arthashastra holds. This undercurrent of the practical economy is also present in the Philosophy of Human Resource Development. The emergence of Human Resource Capital and Human Resource Accounting concepts are the outcome of this undercurrent. D.D. Kosambi has supported the presence of this undercurrent of the practical economy in Arthashastra. He remarked that the state was then the biggest land owner; the sole proprietor of the mining industry; and the biggest producer of all commodities. The state has become powerful as a decisive member of the political administration, acquiring maximum wealth. This economic power is the power of the architecture of the Arthashastra.

There are three kinetic forces that empowered the administrative system in Arthashastra. They are the financial discipline and control over civil servants; prompt revenue recovery and control over expenditure; and motivating and rewarding the civil servants. However, the most important financial discipline in Arthashastra is that where the government is not allowed to spend more than 25% of the total revenue for meeting the expenditure towards the salary and wages of the government. If the expenditure crosses this deadline, it will make the state unstable and unsafe. This is the philosophy behind *Prithvipalanam* (retention of resources). It is a philosophy of natural recycling phenomena of the acquired natural shower of resources through evaporation, humidification and then raining by the solar energy. Broadly to state that 75% of

Figure: 26

People and Conflict Management

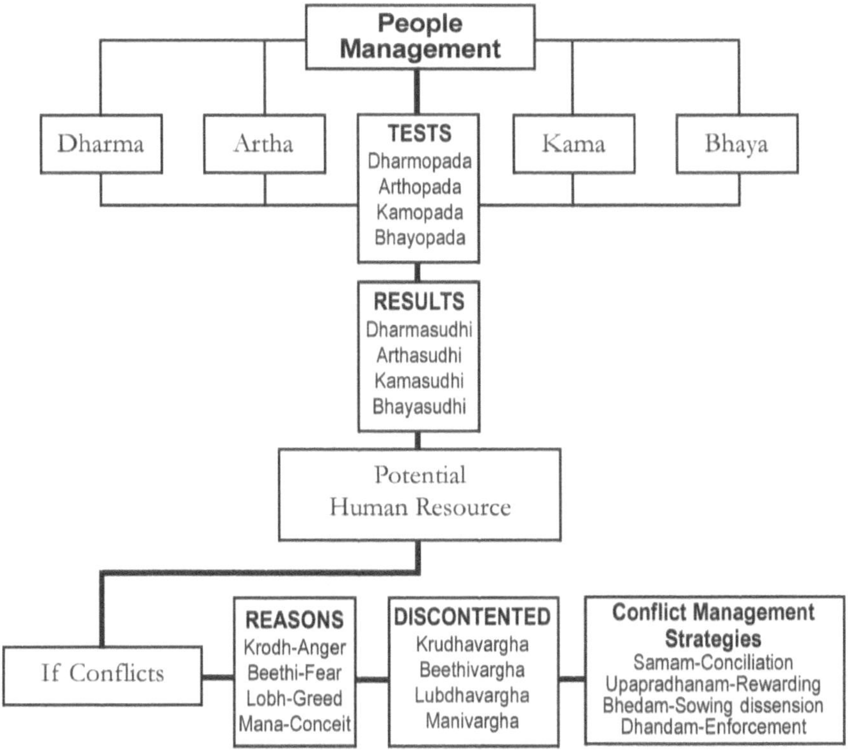

the total revenue collected should be recycled to reach the society after spending a reasonable 25% as operating cost. "The total salary of the state shall be determined in accordance with the capacity of the city and the country side (State) and shall be one quarter of the revenue [25%] of the state. The salary scale shall be such as to enable the accomplishment of state activities (Right people) , shall be adequate for meeting the bodily needs of the state servants and shall not be in contradiction to the principles of *Dharma* and *Artha*" {Bk.5.Ch.3.Vs.1,2.}. This natural justice of recycling is also echoed in *Sri. Chankyanitishastra*: - "O wise man! Give your wealth only to the worthy and never to others. The water of the sea received by the clouds is always sweet. The rain water enlivens all living beings of the earth both movable (insects, animals, humans, etc.) and immovable (plants, trees, etc.), and then returns to the ocean it value multiplied a million fold." {Ch.8.Vs.4} This metaphoric and poetic financial theory of Kautilya is yet to be honored and followed. The latest statistics shows that India has crossed this deadline [only one quarter of the revenue [25%] of the state should be utilized for salary and wages] of expenditure and touched the dangerous range of 85-115%. Consequently the state is under the threat of political instability and economic degeneration.

D.D.Kosambi

Kautilya has depicted a meaningful parable to explain the tendency of the civil servants for corruption. He says that the civil servants are like those who naturally taste the drop that oozed at the tip of the tongue whether it is honey or poison. "Just as it is impossible not to taste honey or poison that one may find at the tip of the tongue, so it is impossible for one dealing with government funds not to taste, at least a little bit, of the king's wealth" {Bk.2.Ch.9.Vs.32.}. Hence, in Arthashastra utmost vigilance was taken to hook up and punish the civil servants who are inclined to corruption and injustice. "Any official who incurs the displeasure of the people shall either be removed from his post or transferred to a dangerous region" {Bk.13.Ch.5.Vs.21.}. There was strict transfer policy and job rotation process so as to mitigate the evils of corruption and injustice.

It is interesting to note that the King himself along with other key officials have timely supervised the civil servants and conducted job evaluation and performance appraisal. Salary was administered on the basis of the level of knowledge and expertise in the respective field of work entrusted to the civil servants. Proper motivation was also seen imparted to increase the performance and productivity of the civil servants and the state. "Appreciation shall be shown, by awarding honours and gifts, to those who are happy with the king [and, therefore loyal]. The discontented shall be tackled by the four methods [conciliation *(Samam)*, placating with rewards and gifts *(Upapradhanam)*, sowing dissension among enemies *(Bhedham)* and enforcement *(Dhanda)*]" {Bk.1.Ch.13.Vs.24-25.}. However it took another 2300 years to constitute an

HRD portfolio and to organize the performance development program in the areas of Human Resource Management. It can be sarcastically commented, that after the Kautilyan period, neither job evaluation nor performance appraisal was carried out as a part of HRD in our civil services or state.

All kinds of employment positions in Arthashastra need sanction from the government. The total ownership and control over employees and employments are vested with the government. Hence, there is no right to any employee either to keep away from the employment or to commit any sort of conscious dysfunction with the employment. Heavy penalty was imposed on those who abstained from employment or defunct the employment. "Wages are paid only for the work done and not for; not doing it" {Bk.3.Ch.14.Vs.2.}. In India, it took another 2300 years to legislate *Dies Non* in its diluted form to restrict salary of those who have abstained from employment and ban *Hartal* in the context of dysfunction with the employment without any justifiable reason.

The concept of work and the worker in Arthashastra does not have any individual existence. They are treated as social asset and economic reality. "With no distraction, people will be fully involved in the work in the fields and there will be an increase in the supply of labour, money, commodities, grain and liquids to the treasury" {Bk.2.Ch.1.Vs.33-35.}. This is the area where Arthashastra differ from the other classics of the Vedic period. While the Vedic literature centralizes the individual interests, Arthashastra centralizes the social and economic interests. Thus the concept of work and the worker obtains the definition of a social asset [work] or an economic reality [worker]; a medium which generate revenue and welfare to the state. Whether it is a work, a project or an enterprise, the main objective should be the generation of wealth. Therefore, Arthashastra insists upon a study of the strict economic feasibility before the execution of a work, a project or an enterprise. Arthashastra also insists upon the human resource discipline, that only those employees who generate or supplement revenue and welfare to the state are to be made permanent [Social Asset]. Those who deplete the treasury or destroy the revenue are terminated from service. There is strong enforcement of law on those who illegitimately generate wealth from the country and accumulate foreign investments. Such people are investigated through the department of espionage or vigilance and if their illegitimacy is proved, they are executed. The recent WikiLeaks revelation of Swiss Bank Accounts of our 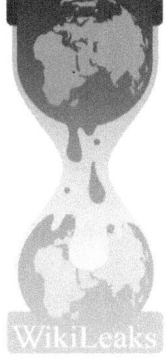 Diplomats, Ministers and Politicians may be recalled in this context.

Financial indiscipline was a major concern in Arthashastra. On the basis of the lapse in financial discipline, Kautilya has classified the civil servants into three. They are Prodigal *(Moolahara)*; the people who squanders his inherited ancestral property in unethical ways, Spendthrift *(Thadhathwika)*; the people who spends whatever he earns as soon as he earns, and

Miserly *(Kadharya)*; the people who amasses wealth and accumulate foreign investments, while making his dependents suffer. In the changed political scenario of the modern world, these three forbidden classes have developed themselves and transformed to a legitimate monopolistic dimension that can be termed as multinational corporate monopoly, political corporate monopoly in public undertakings and transnational corporate monopoly. "In all cases, an official [who has caused loss of revenue to the state] shall not be deprived of his property if he has many dependents [but shall be dismissed from service]. Otherwise, his property shall be confiscated." {Bk.2.Ch.9.Vs.21-22}. In the case of the Miserly *(Kadharya)* "When all facts have been ascertained [by the secret agents], the errant official shall be [falsely] accused [of being in the pay of the enemy] using, as a pretext, a [forged] letter; he shall then be killed" {Bk.2.Ch.9.Vs.27}.

The system of monitoring and preventing corruptions and financial crimes in Arthashastra has a democratized people's participatory function. Arthashastra encouraged people, in addition to the judiciary, to trace out and report the cases of corruptions and financial crimes to the state. Such people are well rewarded by the state. At the same time strict punishments are given to those who fabricate false reports on people as a part of self-interest, political interest or character assassination. "Any informant, to whom an assurance against punishment has been given, shall, if the case is proved, receive (Reward) one sixth of the amount involved; if the informant is a state servant, one-twelfth" {Bk.2.Ch.8.Vs.29.}. "If the case is not proved, the informant shall be given corporal punishment or fined and no mercy shall be shown to him. If an informant withdraws the charge at the instigation of the accused, he shall be condemned to death" {Bk.2.Ch.8.Vs.31, 32.}. In an age of media sensationalism and paid news publishing mechanism, the spirit of Arthashastra is really commendable.

The above anecdote depicts the existence of a fully developed people's court in that period. Hence, it can be concluded that the revolutionary system of people's court recently introduced by the extremists or Naxalites in our country is only the delayed continuation of such a practice recommended in the Arthashastra. It was through this democratic trial, the social or political criminals of that time were crossed publicly and as a part of punishment branded the images of dog, headless torso and female sex organ on their forehead, symbolizing the nature of the offence such as theft, murder and rape respectively; using red-hot metal stamps. "The guilt of the Brahmin shall be displayed publicly and permanently so that he may be excluded from all activities of *Brahmins*. The brand shall indicate the nature of the offence [for theft: dog; for drinking alcoholic liquor: the vintner's flag; for murder: a headless torso; and rape of teachers wife: the female sex organ]. After publicly proclaiming a *Brahmin's* guilt and branding him, he shall be exiled or sent to [work in] the mines" {Bk.4.Ch.8.Vs.28, 29.}. The people's court in Arthashastra would be greatly relevant in the current Indian situation where social justice and femininity is brutally raped.

"Judges shall discharge their duties
objectively and impartially so that they
may earn the trust and affection of
the people"

chapter-8

JUDICIARY AND ARTHASHASTRA

rthashastra in its wider sense is a synthesis of Polity *(Niti)*, Administration *(Dhanda)* and the Management of resources *(Prithvilabham* and *Prithvipalanam)* based on the four sciences or *Shastras* of Philosophy *(Anweeshiki)*. Three *Vedas (Thrayi)*, Economics *(Vartha)* and the science of government *(Dhandaneethi)* are the constituents of *Anweeshiki*. The catalyst in action in the process of this synthesis is the philosophy of *Dharma*. Hence, the study of Arthashastra becomes a complete experience only when one should learn and experience the jurisprudence or *Dharma* synchronized within, as a part of the political administration. The king or the ruler who internalizes this feeling of *Dharma* will automatically gain indefinite power. "A king who administers justice in accordance with *Dharma*, evidence, custom and the written law will be able to conquer the whole world" {Bk.3.Ch.1.Vs.43.}

Though the book has considerable indebtedness to the *Vedic* classics and *Smritis*; in respect of jurisprudence, it has; if not deliberately, a modern legalistic perspective. This perspective rightly reflects the awareness of *Dharmashastra*, the legalistic mind and the judicial thinking of Kautilya. While the *Vedic* classics and *Smritis* respected the social interests, rites and rituals of the privileged classes, Arthashastra protected the all-pervading interests of *Dharma*, in a paternalistic commune beyond class or creed. Besides, it is also evident that the applied *Dharma* in Arthashastra has recovered the lost social identity and social involvement of the *Sudras*. "Because the king is the guardian of the right conduct of this world [*Dharma*] with its four *Varnas* and *Ashramas*, he [alone] can enact and promulgate laws [to uphold them] when all traditional codes of conduct perish [through disuse or disobedience]." {Bk.3.Ch.1.Vs.38.}

This act of regaining of the lost social identity and social involvement of the *Sudras*, is the output that emerged from Kautilya's fervency of criticism against the illicit and fraudulent interpretation of the *Vedic* classics and *Smritis* by the *Brahmin* fanatics and their imposition of those biased code of laws upon the downtrodden and the lower *Varnas*. We have miserably lost this fervency of criticism after Kautil ya's backward journey to the hermi tage; after completing his glorious political mission in Magadha. Centuries later, the imperialists, have commercialized and politicalized those scriptural expressions and made them biased tools of colonial expansion and unleashed the evil spirit of colonization. Thus, they aborted our enriched Sanskrit literature and its voluminous cultural treasures so as to transform them to the meanest of marketable documents.

In consequence of the outbreak of our first independence struggle in 1857, there was the historic in 1858. This was the first recorded political event which commercialized and politicalized the grand Indian culture and tradition. The Doctrine of Lapse was thus introduced in a camouflaged manner, supporting the scriptural expression displayed in *Smritis;* by which the property can be confiscated to the state in the situation where there are no legal masculine heir to inherit the property. This misinterpretation of the *Smritis* signalized the plain exposition of imperialism and it was an unpardonable attack on our glorious culture by the British Imperialists.

The reason for the onslaught of British Imperialism is due to the wrong spirit of domination of the *Brahmins* who monopolized and restricted the education and learning to their own class. As a result of this *Brahmin* Monopoly and spirit of supremacy, the Indian society was disunited and lost its unified effort either to defend or offend the onslaught of the British imperialism. On the other hand, the British who have learned the core sensitive areas of our ethics; have skillfully exploited the integrity of the country. Even though Kautilya has put his green signal for the *Brahmin* domination in the social arena, the study on his system of judiciary nullifies their supremacy in the legal arena. It is very evident that *Dharma* or the state jurisprudence is honoured by all.

8.1. *Arthashastra socialized* Dharma.

This is the context where *Dharmashastra* differ from that of Arthashastra. While the judicial system of the *Dharmashastra* in the Vedic period supports and stabilizes the ritual and spiritual uplift of the King and the *Brahmins*, Arthashastra supports and stabilizes the social as well as the substantial uplift of the people as a whole. According to Dr. Julius Jolly, the general tendency of Arthashastra is that it is thoroughly realistic and worldly, as opposed to the vague idealism and strict religious principles of *Dharmashastra*.

The core of our ancient thought concerning Law was the full recognition of the supremacy of *Dharma* and the clear articulation of the status of *Dharma*, which approximately identifies with the modern concept of the Rule of Law i.e. of all being sustained and regulated by it. The word *Dharma* is clearly derived from the root *'Dhr'*-which denotes: 'upholding', 'supporting', 'nourishing' and 'sustaining'. -that which upholds is *Dharma*. In *Karna Parva* of the *Mahabharata*, the concept of *Dharma* is explained: -"*Dharma* is for the stability of society, the maintenance of social order and the general well-being and progress of humankind. Whatever conduces to the fulfillment of these objects is *Dharma* that is definite". {MBh.Ch.69.Vs.58.}. In *Santi Parva* of the *Mahabharata*, the concept of *Dharma* is connected with the duties of the king: - "The proper function of the King is the maintenance of the law, not enjoying the luxuries of life" {MBh.Ch.90.Vs.3.} "Law only is supreme. So the king who regulates society in fulfillment of the law discharges his functions appropriately" {MBh.Ch.90.Vs.20.}

In ancient days a ruler was not allowed to rule the country the way he like, but was obliged to rule the country according to *Dharma* laid down by the *Shastras,* i.e.:-*Dharmashastra, Arthashastra* and other *Shastra* relating to jurisprudence. The *Dharmashastra* was concerned with the *Dharmic* paths [the right ways] of living. For the preservation of these *Dharmic* paths it had divided the community into several segments and, to ensure that they functioned in unison, it laid down a code of law adhered to *Dharma.* This code of law came into being to establish righteousness, not on-ly for the country as a whole for its day-to-day governance but also for the individual in his day-to-day living. It clearly states that it was the duty of the king to ensure *Dharmic* paths [righteous ways] of life for his people. The state administration was thus considered in the ancient days, a righteous way of living as a part of establishing *Dharma. Shastras,* such as the *Arthashastra* and *Shukra Neet-ishastra* came to be used principally for the maintenance of law and social order and ad-ministration of the state. Yet they all, by and large, followed the *Dharmashastra.*

Dharmachakra

Focusing *Dharma* in the Arthashastra, Kautilya locates it as "The basis for securing and preserving power over the earth." Kautilya emphasize further: 'In the happiness of his subjects lays the king's happiness, in their welfare his welfare. He shall not consider as good only that which pleases him, but treat as beneficial to him whatever pleases his subjects'.

Praja sukhe sukham rajyaha prajanamcha hitehitam
Natma priyam hitam rajnaha prajanam cha hitam priyam.

The Arthashastra code of laws as conceived by Kautilya has been codified in the third *Ad-hikarana* entitled *Dharmastheeyam* which consists of 20 chapters. The judges or magistrates termed as *Dharamasthr* or *Pradheshtr* are recruited through the test, *Dharmopadha* one among the fourfold series of secret tests [*Dharmopadha, Arthopadha, Kamopadha* and *Bhayopadha*] for ensuring *Dharmasudhi.* They were the two classes of judicial officers who harmoniously instituted the judicial system in Arthashastra. Among these *Pradheshtr* (Magistrate) could be seen in *Dharmashastra* but *Dharmasthr* (Judge) is considered to be the own creation of Kauti-lya. In stature they were equated with the *Amathya* and were posted three each in the frontiers and in the administrative centers *Samgrahanam, Dhronamukham* and *Kharvatikam* for the right exercise of the jurisprudence. "There shall be established a bench of three judges who shall hold court at the frontier posts, sub-district headquarters, and provincial headquarters [as neces-sary]. The judges shall be learned in *Dharma* and have the qualifications of a minister

[*Arthasudhi, Dharmasudhi, Kamasudhi* and *Bhayasudhi*]. They shall judge [civil] cases arising from disputes between two parties" {Bk.3.Ch.1.Vs.1.}. Some of the researchers argue that Kautilya engaged these officials as he could not control the judiciary with the help of the King alone when the empire was expanded beyond his control. At the same time it can be derived from this fact that Kautilya has intentionally created an exclusively new position of *Dharmasthr* (Judge) as a part of the democratization of the judiciary i.e. to bring more coverage to judiciary and to decentralize the legal service to the grass root level. *Fig.: 27.*

8.2. The Penal Code of Kautilya.

As in the modern times, cases in Arthashastra are classified into civil and criminal. The civil laws are discussed in the third *Adhikarana, Dharmastheeyam* and the criminal laws are discussed in the fourth *Adhikarana, Kandakasodhanam* of Arthashastra. Civil cases are heard and judged by the *Dharmasthr* as judges and the criminal cases are heard and judged by the *Pradheshtr* as magistrates. Considering the gravity of the cases, there was the Bench system comprised of three judicial officers from among *Dharmasthr, Pradheshtr, Amathya, Samaharthr* or *Adhyaksha*, for hearing and passing judgments. These *Pradheshtrs* (Magistrates) and *Dharmasthrs* (Judges) who passed factual and unbiased judgments have won the hearts of the people. "Judges shall discharge their duties objectively and impartially so that they may earn the trust and affection of the people" {Bk.3.Ch.20.Vs.24.}. Hierarchically, they were placed under the *Samahartrs* and given the status and qualification of the ministers. All the serious cases connected with the temples, priests, blasphemy, *Brahmins* and treason are directly heard and judged by the King himself. Besides, *Amathyas, Samaharthrs* and *Adhyakshas* are also delegated to hear and judge cases according to the gravity and classification. Even though the commandments of the King (*Rajyasasana*) sometimes reach the final verdict (*Anthyasasana*), the King has not been delegated either to frame laws of his own or to break the laws for his own interests. It could be rightly said that the King is institutionalizing his duties towards the state (*Rajyadharma*) where *Dharma* miserably fails. Here the duty of the King is that of the savior of judiciary. Such Kings in Arthashastra are hailed as the almighty of the world and the world beyond and they are also qualified even for canonization. "A king who observes his duty of protecting people justly and according to law will go to heaven, whereas one who does not protect them or inflicts unjust punishment will not." {Bk.3.Ch.1.Vs.41.}. Dr. Julius Jolly has remarked that the detailed descriptions of *Rajyadharma* in *Manu* and *Yajnavalkya* could have been derived from Arthashastra.

There is no doubt in considering the third and fourth *Adhikaranas*; *Dharmastheeyam* and *Kandakasodhanam* respectively are the foundation stones or the indicators of the modern civil and criminal laws. The code of laws in Arthashastra and the code of laws in the modern judiciary are basically the same, in terms of codes, procedures and treatment.

Every case in Arthashastra has four important steps or *Padas*. They are *Dharma* (The truthful actions), *Vyvahara* (The witnesses), *Charithra* (The traditions) and *Sasana* or *Rajyakalpana* (The Royal edicts or commandments of the King). "Any matter in dispute shall be judged according to the four bases of justice. These, in order of increasing importance, are: [*padas*]; *Dharma*, which is based on truth, Evidence, which is based on witnesses [*Vyvahara*]; custom, i.e. the tradition accepted by the people [*Charithra*]; and royal edicts: i.e. law as promulgated [*Sasana* or *Rajyakalpana*]." {Bk.3.Ch.1.Vs.39-40.}. There is a general and predetermined rule for proceeding with the *Dharma* and *Vyavahara*. Hence it is called as the procedural law. There is a positive and definite rule for proceeding with the *Charithra* and *Sasana* or *Rajyakalpana*. Hence it is called as the positive law. Even though it was a period of traditions and the commandments of the King, Kautilya emphasized and supported the procedural system of laws holding the witnesses (*Vyavaharas*) and the predetermined truthful actions (*Dharma*). Unlike supporting documents and proofs Kautilya holds on the sanctity of the witnesses (*Vyavaharas*) and the predetermined truthful actions (*Dharma*). "Whenever there is disagreement between custom and the *Dharma*-

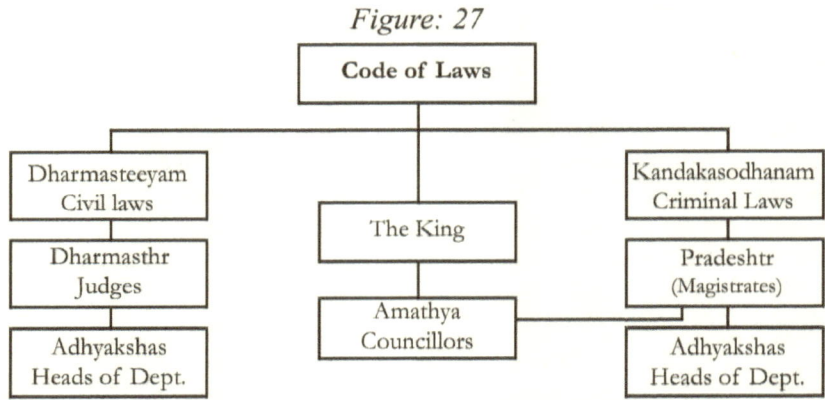

Figure: 27

The structure of Judiciary in Arthashastra

shastras or between the evidence and the *Shastras*, the matter shall be decided in accordance with *Dharma*." {Bk.3.Ch.1.Vs.44.}. This is indeed the democratization of *Dharma* in the judiciary.

One of the important judicial missions of Kautilya is the encouragements, privileges and inspirations he gave to the community of witnesses. While imposing penalty on the fake or countervailing witnesses, Kautilya limits the penalty to between 12 *panas* and 24 *Panas* which is a frugal imposition when compared to others. This is to encourage the community of witnesses and bring them closer to the judiciary. "Witnesses are obliged to tell the truth. For not doing so, the fine shall be 24 *Panas* and half that [*12 Panas*] for refusal to testify." {Bk.3.Ch.11.Vs.49.}. This is the context where Kautilya proved himself a sincere searcher of truth, seer of truth, the protector of truth and a democrat of justice. This aboriginal but genuine code of laws has also proved Arthashastra different from the *Smritis* and *Dharmashastras*.

8.3. The classification of Kautilya code of laws.

The code of laws in Arthashastra has been generally classified into four; such as family laws, contract laws, labour laws and criminal laws and has 17 sections. *Fig: 28.* But on close examination, it can be classified further into six, based on the duties of the king towards the state and duties of the people towards the state. They are (*Rajadharma*), duties of a king towards the people; (*Prajadharma*), duties of people towards the king; [*Kudumbadharma*], the duties towards family; (*Desadharma*), duties of the king and people towards the state; (*Kuladharma*), the duties of people towards the community; and [*Thozhildharma*], the duties of people towards the job. Among the six *Dharmas,* the duties towards family [*Kudumbadharma*] are considered to be the one which has a dominant role in the social fabric. This *Dharma* is dealt in the *Vivahasamyuktham;* the first among the code of laws. This is mainly related to the *Dharma* of *Grihasthashrama.* The *Dharma* of the *Grihastha* – householder - is a prominent phase in every *Arya's* life because it is during this phase that a man contributes to economic activity and maintenance of social order, particularly the perpetuation of his family line. According to Kautilya; "civil transactions begin with marriage." {Bk.3.Ch.2.Vs.1.}. All sorts of civil and criminal disputes arise out of civil transactions. The ultimate objective of the judiciary is therefore the establishment of *Dharma* or righteousness in the individual life (*Swadharmasthapana*) of all classes that extend to the *Dharma* of *Grihasthashrama* and also to the establishment of *Dharma* or righteousness in the royal throne (*Rajyadharmasthapana*).

Accordingly Kautilya gave due weight and significance to the perfect marital relations discussed in the first section (*Vivahasamyuktham*) among the code of laws, as it is the pure source of all *Dharma* and *Adharma*. It is also the cause and effect of all *Dharma* and *Adharma* by which one attain his own ultimate realization of *Dharma* or righteousness (*Sarvadharmasthapana*). The King, who observes and respects all these *Dharma* or righteousness, is able to dominate and rule over the people of the whole world. "A king who observes his duty of protecting his people justly according to law will go to heaven, whereas one who does not protect them or inflicts unjust punishment will not." {Bk.3.Ch.1.Vs.41.}.

Narayan Chandra Bandhyopadhyaya (1927) has rightly commented that "the importance of these laws consists in proving that the early legal system of India was marked by a spirit of rationalism, and this was probably due to the interference of the King who accepting the equitable principles advocated by the jurists of the day, modified thereby the laws to suit the requirements of society and went so far as to suppress unreasonable customs or to repeal them".

8.4. The Judicial Mechanism of Kautilya.

The judicial machinery in Arthashastra is neither the institution of royal tyranny of the past nor the institution of courts in modern times that are stationed in any particular part of the state. But the legal system in Arthashastra is the efficient and dynamic mobile institution of jurisprudence. It makes incessant search for the cases of legal violations among the people and advises prompt and innovative judicial solutions where the old and out of date code of laws have failed. It is very meaningful to note the fact that unlike modern times where judiciary is a highly demanded legal exercise to the people; in Arthashastra, judiciary is a system of voluntary deliverance of legal service to the people.

Figure: 28

Kautilya code of laws.

1.	Vivahasamyuktham	Marriage and allied topics
2.	Dhayavibhagam	Partition of inheritance
3.	Vashthukam	Properties and disputed concerning it
4.	Saamayanapaakarmam	Failure to participate in community affairs
5.	Hrunadhanam	Non payment of deposits
6.	Oupanithikam	Concerning deposits
7.	Dhasakarmakarakalpam	Laws concerning salves and labourers
8.	Sambuyasamuthanam	Undertakings in partnerships
9.	Vikreetha krithanushayam	Revocation of a sale or a purchase
10.	Dhathanapaakarmam	Non conveyance of Gifts made
11.	Aswamivikrayam	Sale without ownership
12.	Saswami sambandham	Laws concerning ownership
13.	Saahasam	Forcible seizure of an object
14.	Vakpaaprushyam	Verbal injury
15.	Dhandapaarushyam	Physical injury
16.	Dhyuthasmaahwayam	Gambiling and challenging
17.	Prakeernakangal	Miscellaneous

In Arthashastra, cases are disposed either by the *Pradheshtr* (Magistrate) or *Dharmastar* (Judge) with immediate effect. Generally, *Pradheshtr* (Magistrate) is entrusted with the hearing and execution of criminal cases and *Dharmastar* (Judge) is entrusted with the hearing and execution of civil cases. They are to "discharge their duties objectively and impartially so that they may earn the trust and affection of the people." {Bk.3.Ch.20.Vs.24.}. If the case is complicated enough to pass judgment in the level of *Pradheshtr* (Magistrate) or *Dharmastar* (Judge), the King will interfere and the case will be settled without any delay. "A judge shall not: threaten, intimidate, drive away or unjustly silence any litigant; abuse any person coming before the court; fail to put any relevant and necessary questions or ask any irrelevant or unnecessary ones; leave out relevant answers to his questions; remind any facts; draw attention to an earlier statement; fail to call for relevant evidence; call for irrelevant evidence; decide on a case without calling any evidence; dismiss a case under some [biased] pretext; make someone abandon the case [purposefully]; misrepresent a statement; coach witnesses; and rehear a case which had been completed and judgment pronounced. All these are punishshable offences; in case the offence is repeated, the judge shall be fined double and removed from office." {Bk.4.Ch9.Vs.13-16.}. There is no question of appealing the cases in a hierarchical manner to various courts such as lower court, high court, Supreme Court and the president's office as we do in modern times. The legal service in Arthashastra is very much tangible, open and democratic; and the judgment final.

The other strategic fact to notice is that there are no advocates or advocate clerks to commercialize the legal service in Arthashastra. This glorifies the Philosophy of Kautilya insisting, that such a kind of extreme commercialization should not be allowed to exist in the state as a means of acquisition [*Prithvilabham*] of material resources [wealth]. At the same time the judicial machinery that comprised of the *Pradheshtr* (Magistrate) or *Dharmastar* (Judge) are engaged as official instruments to collect the revenue of the state. The statutory application of the norms of penalty and the imposition of penalty for non-remittance or late-remittance of taxes, are exercised by them as legal officials. This utilization of the judicial machinery as recovery machinery of the state revenue shows the practical *Sutra* of judiciary and financial administration of the state as designed by Kautilya. "[The judges and] magistrates shall determine whether to levy the highest, the middle or lowest penalty [in the prescribed scale] taking into account the person sentenced, the nature and gravity of the offence, the motive and circumstances prevailing [at the time of offence], as well as the consequences while maintaining a balance between the interest of the king [i.e. the state] and the individual [i.e. the people]." {Bk.4.Ch. 10.Vs.17-18.}.

The most popular statement that the innocent should not be punished under any circumstances even if a thousand criminals escape from punishments; is a justifiable and practically true statement in Arthashastra. Unlike in the modern times, there is no chance of the innocent denied of legal justice or punished in Arthashastra. There justice is neither denied nor delayed. If proved otherwise, the legal machinery involved; *Pradheshtr* (Magistrate), *Dharmasthr* (Judge), Judge's clerk or even the King; will be punished in a deserving manner for being instrumental to the denial or delay of justice. The punishment on such occasion, is double the punishment and penalty imposed on the innocent. If the gravity of the judicial lapse is found serious, the person responsible for the lapse; is suspended from the state service. Therefore "the *Pradheshtr* (Magistrate) or *Dharmasthr* (Judge) shall not: impose a fine when it is not prescribed; impose a fine higher or lower than the prescribed one; award physical punishment when it is not prescribed; disallow a just claim; and allow an unjust claim." {Bk.4.Ch.9.Vs.18-20.}. Arthashastra has generalized three such judicial lapses. They are as follows: -

1) To make the respondent either accused or innocent without any legal reasonability.

2) The illegal conduct of untimely and unwanted cross-questioning.

3) To grant illegal concessions, helps and extension of time to earn and influence witnesses.

8.5. *Vivahasamyuktham and Sexual liberalization.*

As explained earlier, marital relations and the co-related *Dharma* codified as *Vivahasamyukatham,* is the prominent among the Arthashastra code of laws. The ultimate goal of marital relations is the fruition of *Grihasthashrama.* But Kautilya deliberately deviates from his own architectural style of composition of the book and makes a strategic turn to the law code of *Smritis.* This is to support the mobilization of a masculine force to prove the philosophy of *Prithvilabham* and *Prithvipalanam.* Keeping an affirmed footage on the *Smritis,* Kautilya philosophizes that the *raison d'être* of a woman is to beget a boy. "The aim of taking a wife is to beget sons" {Bk.3.Ch.2.Vs.42.}. The freedom of women, as acclaimed in Arthashastra is really the covert form of a sort of sexual liberalization to multiply the masculine force. It is this masculine force that makes the philosophy of *Prithvilabham* (Acquisition of territory) and *Prithvipalanam* (Retention of the acquired territory) practically workable. Quite evidently; against the core philosophy of Kautilya, the colour scheme, caste system, the rites and rituals and other scriptural taboos are seen sabotaged to grant sexual liberalization to women. So liberalized was Arthashastra in the areas of marriage, divorce, remarriage, inter-caste and inter-colour scheme marriages, women's right to property and other rules of inheritance. This allowance of freedom of women or sexual liberalization in Arthashastra has been widely criticized and Kautilya has been accused as a women-hater. But the criticism and allegation are countered by the argument that Kautilya's main motive behind the sexual liberalization is the multiplication and mobilization of a powerful masculine force to uphold the philosophy of *Prithvilabham* (Acquisition of territory) and *Prithvipalanam* (Retention of the acquired territory). Frenzied on his philosophy, Kautilya has extended the sexual liberalization allowing women to have sex with even lepers or mad men to beget a boy if her husband is unable to do so. "A husband is not obliged to have intercourse with a wife who is either insane or a leper. However, a wife can have intercourse with a leprous or mad husband, in order to beget a son." {Bk.3.Ch.2.Vs.45-47.}. In the same manner a girl who has attained puberty has been given the right and freedom to marry the man she likes even against the rules of the colour scheme and caste system. "It shall not be an offence for a daughter, remaining unmarried for three years after her first menstruation, to marry a man of the same *Varna,* and she shall be free to marry a man of [even] another *Varna* provided that she does not take with her the ornaments. [given by her father]." {Bk.4.Ch1.2.Vs.10.}. The father of the girl will be punished for he has abstained from his duty of getting his daughter married in time.

Indian Wedding

- 100 -

8.6. Guilds *and the labour Laws.*

There is ample evidence to show that Arthashastra has protected and managed the Human Resource Capital of the time. There existed a kind of cooperative local bodies called *Guilds* to control and manage the working class and their work culture. The *Guilds* formed by the self-employed artisans and craftsmen guaranteed the character and conduct of its members, mode of delivery of goods and the quality of the goods. {Bk.4.Ch.1.Vs.2-3.}. The *Guilds* controlled by *Amathya* or *Pradheshtr* can be equated with the present concept of trade unions or labour tribunals/courts. The working capital for the maintenance of such *Guilds* is collected from the workers as membership fees. This further proves that there existed a statutory employee-employer relationship in Arthashastra like our modern Check off System which some of our modern corporate managements still hesitate to implement. These *Guilds* ensured a healthy working environment, employee welfare and very good employee-employer relationship and participatory function.

The other labour laws existed in Arthashastra are as follows: -

1) To have one-tenth of the profit share, is an eligible right of the employee. This can be given either in cash or kind.

2) Right to punish the employee who abstains from work.

3) Right to punish the employer who does not pay for the work. In such cases penalty is ten times the salary of the employee.

4) Not to be employed in unhealthy environment.

5) Not to be employed for killing.

6) Not to employ children.

7) Right for holidays. If employee is made to work on holidays, double the wages should be paid.

8) Right to employment for the orphan and the helpless women.

9) Right to employment and other welfare allowances for the dependent of the employee who dies while on duty.

In brief, it may be concluded that the judiciary in Arthashastra is the practical workout of the social virtues based on the *Dharma* (The truthful actions), *Vyvahara* (The witnesses). Justice in Arthashastra is not the final victory based on the invincible dominance of any arguments or counter arguments in the court room, but the exposition of the luminous *Dharmic* reflections that come out of ultimate truth and justice.

"The *Samahartr* (The administrator) shall be always diligent in administering the *Janapada* [countryside] and shall employ the [appropriate] secret agents to ensure that servants of the state perform their duties."

chapter-9

SOCIAL SECURITY IN ARTHASHASTRA

The total security system and the foreign policy management in Arthashastra are integrated and discussed in the *Kandakasodhanam*, the fourth *Adhikarana* of the book. This *Adhikarana* deals with the social security, state security, foreign policy management and the criminal laws in detail through its thirteen chapters. The title of this *Adhikarana* itself is highly communicative and indicates the central thought-process of Arthashastra. *Kandaka* means thorns; the thorns of social evils. *Sodhana* means the removal or eradication; the eradication of social evils. *Kandakasodhanam* ascertains a clean society free from social evils and a secure society free from social criminals. The social security centers for the process of *Kandakasodhanam* are established in all *Samgrahanam, Kharvatigham, Dhronamukam, Sthaneeyam* and frontier provinces. "There shall be established a bench of three judges who shall hold court at frontier posts, sub-district headquarters, and provincial headquarters [as necessary]." {Bk.3.Ch.1.Vs.1.}.

The responsibility of the total security system in Arthashastra is vested upon the *Samahartrs*. However their responsibility is more concentrated especially in the security system of the villages. "The *Samahartr* (The administrator) shall be always diligent in administering the *Janapada* [countryside] and shall employ the [appropriate] secret agents to ensure that servants of the state perform their duties." {Bk.2.Ch.35.Vs.15.}. *Samahartrs* were further assisted by the *Pradhesters* who are in charge of the security of the fortified towns and districts. In addition to this the *Sthanikas*; the district administrators, *Nagarikas*; the city administrators, *Gramikas*; the heads of villages, *Anthapalas*; the protectors of frontiers and the *Adavikas*; the heads of hill tribes have also assisted the *Samahartrs* and maintained the law and order situations in Arthashastra. While the *Samahartr* (The administrator) secures and controls the life in *Janapada* [countryside], *Nagarika* (the city administrator) secures and controls the life in the cities. "*Nagarika*, the city administrator shall be responsible for: control over charitable lodging houses and ensuring that visitors to the city stay at the places specified for them [Migration control]; control over trade, particularly sale at fair prices and prevention of sale of stolen goods [trade and commerce control]; maintenance of law and order, particularly observance of curfew regulations [law and order control]; ensuring observance of fire precautions and providing firefighting equipment [fire control]; ensuring cleanliness and sanitation, including control over cremation grounds [health control]; prisons [Prison control]; and custody of lost property [theft control]." {Bk.2.Ch.36.Vs.5-39, 43-47.}. *Fig: 29, 30.*

The other instruments working in the security system to help *Samahartrs* are the spies under the cover of intelligence officer *(Kapatika)*; monks *(Udhasthitha)*; householders *(Grihapati kavyajna)*; merchants *(Vydhehakavyajna)*; ascetics *(Thapasa vyajna)*; the secret agent *(Sathrin)*; the assassin *(Theekshna)*; the Poisoners *(Rasadha)*; the women mendicant *(Bhikshuki)*; and those who drive out thieves *Chorarajukas*. These instruments form an infallible democratic network of the central security system. It is this security network that hooked up the undesirable anti-social elements and paraded them in public so as to punish justifiably. "When thieves and robbers are arrested, the *Samahartr* [The administrator] shall parade them before the people of the city or the countryside [as the case may be] and proclaim that the criminals were caught under the instructions of the king, an expert in detecting thieves. The people shall be warned to keep under control any relative with criminal tendencies, because all thieves were bound to be caught [like the ones paraded before them]." {Bk.4.Ch.5.Vs.13.}. This public parading, works two-fold in the public conscience; one is to make aware the social psyche that the security system of the state is alert; and the second is to remind the people of the king's omniscience. These elements of social security system are, no doubt, obliged to a strong centralized Monarchy and also become instrumental for the existence of an unquestionable Monarch. The secret of success of the central security system in Arthashastra is this instrumental attachment to the monarchy. Fig: 18. The three important facts on which Kautilya's concept of centralized Monarchy stands are as follows:

1) The King is never enslaved to the people.

2) The state and the supreme power are one.

3) No Monarch is made benevolent due to the influence of the limitations of the constitution or due to the challenge against him. In fact the reason for his benevolence is due to his knowledge of *Dharmashastra* and also due to his instinct to be self-defended.

9.1. *Kosadhandabala: The power of Money and Monarch.*

This spirit of centralized monarchy forces the King for the empowerment of treasury *(Artha)* and army *(Dhanda)*. After accumulating sufficient money from all the available means (enriched *Kosa*), the King concentrates on the empowerment of the army (enriched *Dhanda*) through the militarism of the chief officers like *Ayudhagaradhyaksha, Pathyadhaksha, Aswadhyaksha, Hasthyadhyaksha, Rathadhyaksha* and *Navadhyaksha*. This contributes to the general structural power of the state (power of *Kosadhanda or Kosadhandabalam*). Besides, the traditional power *(Moulabalam)*, the national power *(Bruthakabalam)*, people's power *(Srenibalam)*, the power of the ally *(Mithrabalam)* and the power of the hired army *(Amithrabalam)* are also supplements of sufficient power to the King.

The total security system and the foreign policy management as conceived by Kautilya in Arthashastra are designed in tune with his own *Mandala* theory. According to this theory of

Mandala or circle, every state has its own internal structural attitudes such as enemy attitude *(Aribhavam)*, ally attitude *(Mithrabhavam)* and national attitude *(Bruthakabhavam)*. The working of the *Mandala* theory is based upon these internal structural attitudes.

Figure: 29

Administration of the Countryside

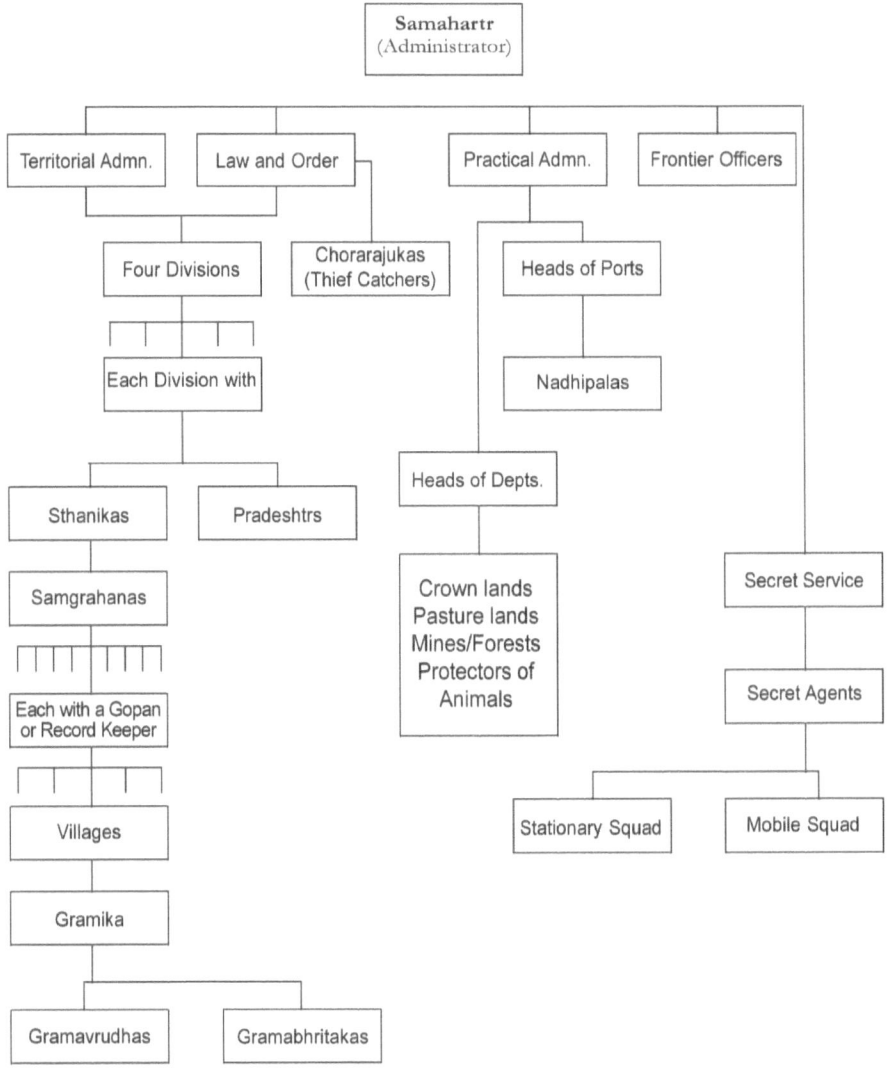

The design of the *Mandala* or circle theory *(Rajyamandalathathwa)* of Kautilya is based upon the concept of small state with a common frontier and focusing on a conqueror *(Vijigishu)*. According to the assumption of Kautilya, the conqueror *(Vijigishu)* is the king who wants to win or to become the 'would be conqueror'. A neighbouring king is then designated as 'the enemy', and other kings nearby as 'allies', a middle king and a neutral king. The emphasis to be considered here is that the conqueror is not necessarily 'a good king' and, correspondingly, the enemy 'a bad king'. The advice given to the conqueror can equally be applied to the enemy. It was from this hypothesis that Kautilya developed his theory of *Rajyamandala*. Hence, Kautilya is rightfully known as the great diplomatic theorist of the inter-state relations and the inter-state power dynamism. The books titled *Shadgunyam* {Bk.7.}, *Sanghavrutham* {Bk.11.} and *Abaliasm* {Bk.12.} together constitute a brilliant, comprehensive, cohesive and logical analysis of all aspects of the inter-state relations and the inter-state power dynamism. The theory of *Rajyamandala* stands on two basic facts that; (i). An immediate neighbouring state is an enemy and (ii). A neighbour's neighbour; separated oneself by the intervening enemy, is a friend.

Figure: 30

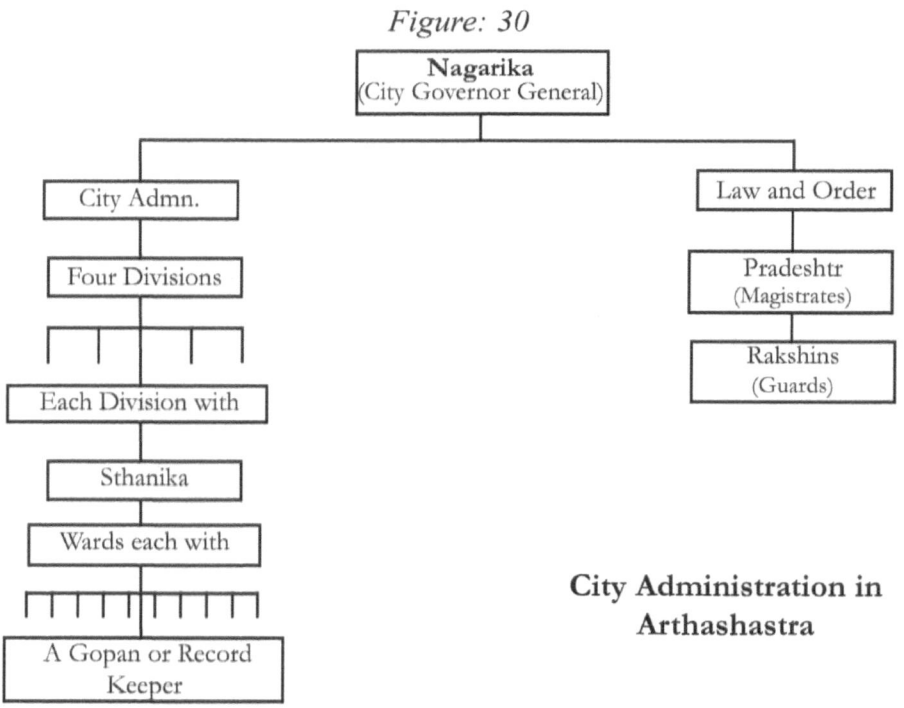

City Administration in Arthashastra

This theory recognizes of twelve states *(Rajyamandala)* classified into two, consists of five states each, as (1) the *Mandala* of enemy *(Arimandala)* and (2) the *Mandala* of ally *(Mithramandala)*. The *Mandala* of bargain or horse trade will consist of two *Mandalas* such as the *Mandala* of the middle King *(Madhyamam)* and the neutral King *(Udhaseenam)*.

Thus the total internal constituents of the state come to twelve. The *Mandala* of enemy *(Arimandala)* from the top to bottom position is: 1. Enemy's ally friend *(Arimithramithram)*. 2. Enemy's ally *(Arimithram)*. 3. Enemy *(Ari)*-Middle position. 4. Rear enemy *(Parshnygrahan)*. 5. Rear enemy's ally *(Parshnygrahasaran)*. The *Mandala* of ally *(Mithramandala)* from the top to bottom position is: 1. Friend of the ally *(Mithramithram)*. 2. Ally *(Mithram)*. 3. Conqueror *(Vijigishu)* -Middle position. 4. Rear ally *(Akrandhan)*. 5. Rear ally's friend *(Akrandhasaran)*. The *Mandala* of bargain or horse trade from left to right position is: 1.The middle King *(Madhyamam)* - left position. 2. The neutral King *(Udhaseenam)* - right position. Fig: 20.

Among these twelve states in the *Rajyamandala* all except the middle King *(Madhyamam)* and the neutral King *(Udhaseenam)* are equally powerful. The *modus operandi* of the *Mandala* theory is that the *Mandala* of the enemy *(Arimandala)* will be active when the Rear enemy *(Parshnygrahan)*, the heel catcher, holds the Conqueror *(Vijigishu)* from the back. Watching this, the Real ally *(Akrandhan)* cries out for the help of the Conqueror *(Vijigishu)* and the *Mandala* of the ally *(Mithramandala)* become active. Both the middle King *(Madhyamam)* and the neutral King *(Udhaseenam)* will act as the *Mandala* of bargain or horse trade amidst the power -play between the *Arimandala* and *Mithramandala*. This is the pivotal source of the power of allies, the power of enemies and the power of horse trading, that keeps the states in peaceful political equilibrium.

9.2. Shadgunyam and the Ten Political Facts derived.

For the perfect maintenance of this peaceful political equilibrium Kautilya has framed a six-fold theory of political balancing *(Shadgunyathathwa)* in the *Adhikarana, Kandakasodhanam.* {Bk.7.}. "Some teachers say that the six methods are; making peace *(Sandhi)*, waging war *(Vigraham)*, doing neither [*Sandhi* nor *Vigraham*] *(Asanam)*, preparing for war *(Yanam)*, seeking protection *(Samsrayam)* and adopting a duel policy [of either *Sandhi* or *Vigraham.*] *(Dwaithabhavam)*. Vatavyadhi [however] says that there are only two methods-waging wars and making peace, because the others are only derivatives of these two. Kautilya agrees [with the view] that there are indeed six methods because each one is applicable in a different set of circumstances." {Bk.7.Ch.1.Vs.2-5} *Fig: 31.*

The six-fold theory can be explained as follows: -

1) If weak, make peace treaty *(Sandhi)*

2) If strong, wage war *(Vigraham)*

3) If equally strong, stay quiet *(Asanam)*

4) If very strong, prepare for war *(Yanam)*

5) If very weak, seek support from others *(Samsrayam)*

6) Strong, if acquire strength from outside *(Dwaithabhavam)*; consists of either *Sandhi* or *Vigraham.*

Figure: 31

Six-fold theory of political equilibrium

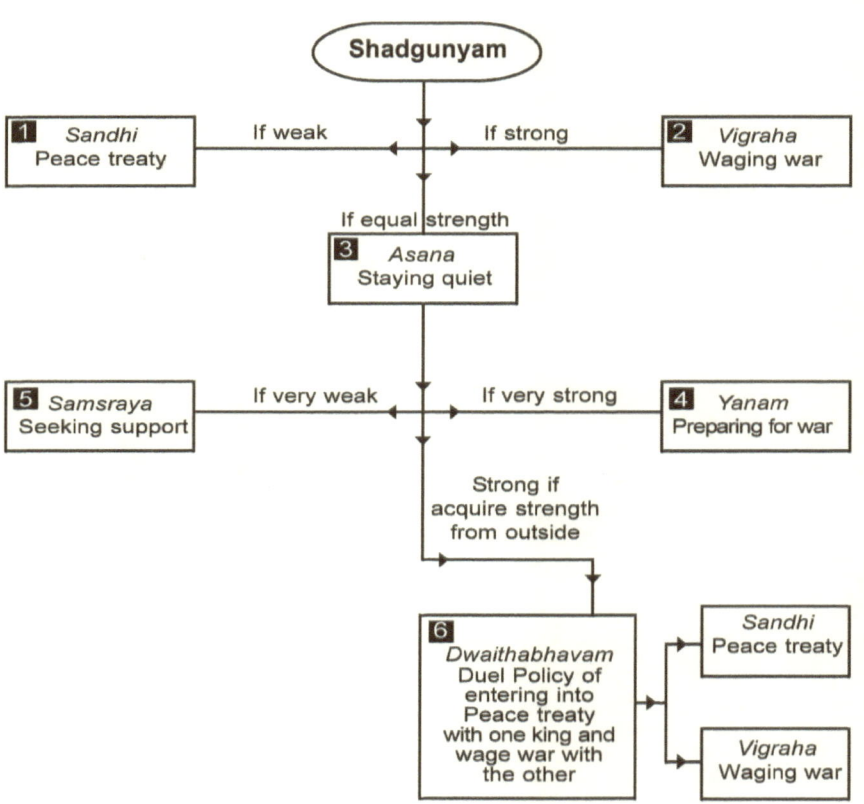

The *Mandala* theory and the correlated six-fold theory *(Shadgunyam)* for maintaining the inter-state relations and power dynamism to attain peaceful political equilibrium among states, helps the strong and weak states as well. It helps the strong for expediting the expansion of the state [not in the sense Colonization] through acquisition of territories *(Prithvilabham)* and helps the weak for protecting the acquired territories from the threat of imperialists *(Prithvipalanam)*.

The application of this six-fold theory *(Shadgunyam)* to uphold the inter-state relations, the power dynamism and the political equilibrium can be evidently seen in modern world history. The defeat of Germany during the First World War and the resurrection of the same Germany during the Second World War is a good example for the practical application of the six-fold theory *(Shadgunyam)* of the inter-state relations, the power dynamism and the political equilibrium.

As stated by A. L. Bhasham that "Arthashastra knows nothing about fair play in battle. Arthashastra earnestly looks on conquest of the demoniac variety as the most profitable and advisable"; we could not see a humane or justifiable attack or warfare in Arthashastra. The attack or warfare in Arthashastra on the other hand is diabolically cruel enough for barbaric killings and other heinous activities. Footing firmly on the rigid principles of acquisition *(Prithvilabham)* and retention of the acquired *(Prithvipalanam)*, we could not expect either humane or moral approach towards attack or warfare in Arthashastra; for it is a manual of imperial polity. The aim of the philosophy of Kautilya is not to explore and uphold the morality in the process of territorial acquisition, but to make the philosophy practical on the principles of acquisition *(Prithvilabham)* and retention of the acquired *(Prithvipalanam)*. But noteworthy to state, that there was strict compliance of prior specifying of the place and time of the battle in accordance with *Dharma*, to prove the saying: *Dharmishta yudhah:* This shows the military ethics of Kautilya. "To be in accordance with *Dharma*, the place and time of battle must be specified beforehand" {Bk.10.Ch.3.Vs.26.}. Hence the allegation against the lapse of morality in warfare does not stand and the alleger has no moral right for expecting such a fair battle from Kautilya.

A. L. Bhasham

R.P. Kangle, in this context, has rightly commented that, "the dream that politics may be thoroughly ethical may perhaps be realized in some future date. It is however unfair in the meanwhile to condemn an author of over 2000 years ago; an author, moreover frankly the most practical and realistic who ever wrote on this subject, for not recommending something that is found impractical in politics even today". *(Kangle R.P., The Kautilya Arthashastra, 2000, Part*

III, P.265.). Besides, it is a living fact indeed that the modern civilized countries even after 2300 years are not maintaining much fairness or ethics in their deals over internal conflicts and warfare.

The experimented and proven facts of the applied six-fold theory *(Shadgunyam)* of the inter-state relations, the power dynamism and political equilibrium are summarized as follows: -

1) An immediate neighbouring state is an enemy.

2) A neighbour's neighbour; separated oneself by the intervening enemy, is a friend.

3) The power is not a factor which is constant over time.

4) The king shall develop his state, i.e. augment its resources and power in order to enable him to embark on a campaign of conquest.

5) The enemy shall be eliminated to attain ultimate success.

6) Those who help in crisis are friends.

7) Always choose the course of prudence.

8) Peace is to be preferred to war.

9) The King's behaviour, in victory and defeat, must be just.

10) Life with the one, who has come from the enemy camp, is like living with a poisonous snake.

Now it is high time to unleash the un-conquerable spirit of Kautilya once again. I unleash the warhorse. It is the moral responsibility of the global citizen to curb the spirit of this exceptional gene

chapter-10

KAUTILYA UNLEASHED

Kautilya offered a complete conceptual framework and a set of concrete policy measures to promote administrative paternalism and socio-economic development. He specifically emphasized far-sighted innovations in political administration adhering to the theory of Acquisition (*Prithvilabham*) and Retention of resources (*Prithvipalanam*) through the observance of Indian philosophy. Kautilya conveyed the importance of virtue ethics and proved that they were sources of 'joy and bliss'. He based his discourse primarily on action-oriented ethical principles and vigorously projected them as essential to the maintenance of law and order, and to the promotion of administrative paternalism and socio-economic development.

In the light of these inferences, I hope this book has indubitably proved that the Modern Management theories specifically in the areas of Human Resource Management and Development (HRM & HRD) and Finance Management (FM) must have been either inherited or germinated from the land of Kautilya (321 BC-298 BC). I also hope that the book has also proved that the Indian philosophy of *Purushartha* (*Dharma, Artha, Kama* and *Moksha*) has to be the bed-rock for the architecture of all developmental strategies of nations and organizations. The value of human resource and *Artha* (Material resources) is also proved to be quantitatively and qualitatively identical in all aspects and efforts should be taken to *acquire* and *retain* the resources without any segregation. The relevance of Agro-Industrial Economics and a Socialistic pattern of society are also highly emphasized and recommended by the great visionary Kautilya.

I hope the comparative study and analysis I conducted in this book have shown that all the components of management that related to the *Acquisition* and *Retention* of human resources and *Artha* (Material resources) were structured, designed, tested and applied successfully by Kautilya centuries ago, through the Indian philosophy of *Prithvilabham* (Acquisition) and *Prithvipalanam* (Retention). So also it has doubtlessly been ascertained that the fundamental theory of judiciary, social security system and political administration of modern society had its roots in the *Aryavartha* of Kautilya.

The eminent research scholar Johann Mayor who has done immense research studies in Sanskrit Literature and Arthashastra says that *Kautaleeyam* (Arthashastra) is not a single book, but a compendium of books. At least twenty years of research and a minimum of five hundred times of his intelligence is needed for a scholar to give a satisfactory commentary on Arthashastra to modern society.

Johann Mayor, no doubt, is an expert captain who sail the giant warship in the expansive ocean of Sanskrit Literature and I am but a small child who floats a paper boat in the trivial tributary that is far away from that great ocean. Hence, I could not claim that this complete but incomplete study will give you an exceptional micro perspective of Arthashastra, I am happy enough to leave the rest of my research to the scholars of posterity.

Kautilya is not a legendary figure of past history. He is but a historic revolutionary and visionary movement that retranslated and reinterpreted ancient Indian thought and philosophy. His revolutionary and visionary strategies of political administration, even now, could provide new knowledge and pragmatic ideas amidst the innumerable modern revolutions and visions that are yet to be proved and made productive.

Now it is high time to unleash the unconquerable spirit of Kautilya once again. I unleash the warhorse. It is the moral responsibility of the global citizen to curb the spirit of this exceptional gene and to determine the genesis of posterity and a new world of welfare.

GLOSSARY

Adavikar: A type of tribe in Arthashastra

*Adhikaranas: The name given to sections of Arthashastra.
There are 15 Adhikaranas.*

Adhyakshas: Heads of the Departments

Akaradhyaksha: Chief controller of mining and metallurgy

Akrandhan: Real ally (Theory of Mandala)

Akrandhasaran: Rear ally's friend (Theory of Mandala)

Akshapadaladhyaksha: Chief controller of accounts and audit

Amithrabalam: The power of the hired army

Amitram: Enemy (Theory of Mandala)

Anaryagana: The community of Non Aryans

Antavasayika: A type of tribe in Arthashastra

Anthyasasana: The final verdict (The code of laws)

Anweeshiki: The Philosophy (HRD)

Aribhavam: Enemy attitude (Theory of Mandala)

Ari: Enemy (Theory of Mandala)

Arimithram: Enemy's ally (Theory of Mandala)

Arimithramithra: Enemy's ally friend (Theory of Mandala)

Arishadwarghas: Six senses or enemies within a person

Artha: The wealth or Resources of material well-being (Economics)

Arthasudhi: The cultural purity of Artha (The fourfold test-HRD)

*Arthopada: One of the fourfold test to test whether the duty
consciousness towards one's country has been sacrificed for mere material gain. (HRD)*

Aryagana: The community of Aryans

Asanam: Staying quiet (Theory of Shadgunyam)

Aswadhyaksha: Chief Commander of cavalry

Athyayam: Fine and penalties (Economics)

Ayamukham: Main heads of accounts of revenue (Economics)

Ayasareeram: Main body of revenue accounts (Economics)

Ayudhagaradhyksha: Chief of Ordinance

Ayudheeyam: Revenue collected through Administrator (Economics)

Baheerika: A type of tribe in Arthashastra

Bandhanagaradhyaksha: Chief Superintendent of jail

Bhagam: Share of production (Economics)

Bhayasudhi: The cultural purity of Bhaya (The fourfold test-HRD)

Bhayopada: One of the fourfold test to test whether the duty consciousness towards one's country feared of evil and rebel forces. (HRD)

Bhedham: Sowing dissension among enemies (Conflict Management-HRD)

Bheethivargha: Discontented people of fear (Conflict Management-HRD)

Bhikshuki: Spies under the cover of the women mendicant (Espionage)

Brahmin: The elite and privileged class in Arthashastra

Bruthakabala: The national power

Bruthakabhava: National attitude

Chandala: A type of tribe in Arthashastra

Charithra: The traditions (The Code of laws)

Chaturvarnya: Four-Varna scheme prevailed in ancient India

Chorarajukas: Those drives out the thieves; connected with the department of espionage

Desadharma: Duties towards state (The Code of laws)

Devadhadhyaksha: Chief Superintendent of temples

Dhanda: Army

Dhandaneethi: The code of punishment to control commitment of sins, crimes and other mistakes or the science of government

Dharamasthar: Judges in Arthashastra (The Code of laws)

Dharma: The truthful actions (The Code of laws)

Dharmasudhi: The cultural purity of Dharma (The fourfold test-HRD)

Dharmopada: One among fourfold test to test the duty consciousness towards one's country and its people. (HRD)

Dhravyaprakriti: Sixty material constituents (Theory of Mandala)

Dhronamukham: Administrative center for four hundred villages

Dhuthadhyaksha: Chief controller of gambling

Durgam: Fortified Town

Dwaithabhavam: Application of duel policy of Sandhi and Vigraham (Theory of Shadgunyam)

Dwarabaheerika: A type of tribe in Arthashastra

Ganikadhyaksha: Chief controller of entertainers and brothels

Ghani: Mines

Ghanyadhyaksha: Chief Superintendent of mines

Gopan: Thahasildar

Gothram: Tribe

Govadhyaksha: Chief Superintendent of crown herds

Gramavrudhas: Village Elders

*Grihapatikavyajna: Spies under the cover of householders
(Espionage)*

Grihasthashrama: The Ashrama of the house holder

*Guilds: A cooperative local body to control and manage the working class and their work culture
(HRD)*

Harsha: Foolhardiness (HRD)

Hasthyadhyaksha: Chief Commander of elephant corps

Indriyajaya: Control over five senses (HRD)

Janapada: Countryside

*Kadharya: People who illegitimately earn the national wealth and make foreign investments.
(Economics)*

Kama: The Lust (HRD)

Kamasudhi: The cultural purity of Karma (Fourfold test-HRD)

*Kamopada: One of the fourfold test to test whether the duty
consciousness towards one's country has been sacrificed for mere physical pleasures. (HRD)*

Kandakasodhanam: The fourth Adhikarana of Arthashastra

Kapatika: Spies under the cover of intelligence officer (Espionage)

Karam: Tax in cash (Economics)

Kautaleeyam: The other name for Arthashastra

Kharvatikam: Administrative centre for two hundred villages

Kliptham: Fixed Charges (Economics)

Kosa: Treasury (Economics)

Kosadhyakshan: Chief Superintendent of treasury

Koshtagaradhyaksha: Chief Superintendent of warehouse

Krodh: Anger (HRD)

*Krudhavargha: Discontented people of anger
(Conflict Management-HRD)*

Kshathriya: The class that are privileged to serve in the army in Arthashastra

Kudumbadharma: Duties towards family (The code of laws)

Kuladharma: Duties towards community (The code of laws)

Kupyadhyaksha: Chief Superintendent of forest produce

Kutalan: Name of a tribe to which Kautilya belong to.

Lakshanadhyaksha: Chief Master of the mint

Lavanadhyaksha: Chief salt commissioner

Lobh: Greed (HRD)

Lohadhyaksha: Chief Superintendent of metals

Lubdhavargha: Discontented people of greed
(Conflict Management-HRD)

Madhyamam: The middle King (The theory of Mandala)

Mahamatras: The 18 Theerthas inherited from ancient Shastras.

Mana: conceit (HRD)

Manadhyaksha: Chief surveyor and time keeper

Mandala theory: The great theory circle of states by Kautilya

Manivargha: Discontented people of conceit
(Conflict Management)

Mithrabalam: The power of the ally (The theory of Mandala)

Mithrabhavam: Ally attitude (The theory of Mandala)

Mithram: Ally (The theory of Mandala)

Mithramithram: Friend of the ally (The theory of Mandala)

Mlecha: A type of tribe in Arthashastra

Moolaharar: People who spoil the paternal wealth. (Economics)

Moulabalam: The traditional power

Mudhradhyaksha: Chief passport officer

Mudhrarakshasam: The Sanskrit play based on Kautilya written by Visakadhathan

Mulyam: Cost Price (Economics)

Nagavanadhyaksha: Chief elephant forester

Navadhyaksha: Chief controller of shipping

Pada: Steps (The code of laws)

Panchendriya: Five senses (HRD)

Panyadhyaksha: Chief controller of state trading

Parigham: Monopoly Tax (Economics)

Parshnygrahan: Rear enemy (The theory of Mandala)

Parshnygrahasaran: Rear enemy's ally (The theory of Mandala)

Parswam: Surcharges (Economics)

Pashandar: A type of tribe in Arthashastra

Pashandavasa: A type of tribe in Arthashastra

Patanadhyaksha: Chief controller of ports and harbors

Pathyakshan: Chief of commander of infantry

Pindakaram: Tax paid in kind from villages (Economics)

Pouthavadhyaksha: Chief controller of weights and measures

Pradheshtr: Magistrates in Arthashastra (The code of laws)

Prajadharma: Duties towards the people (The code of laws)

Prakaranas: The name given to the sub sections in the chapters under Adhikaranas in Arthashastra.

Prakrayam: Royalty (Economics)

Prakriti Sampath: People provided with prosperity and welfare. (Human Asset-HRD)

Prakriti: Those people who give tax to the King and other people that serve the King. (Human resource-HRD)

Prathikaram: Tax compensated as cash/kind/HR (Economics)

Prithvilabham: Acquisition of resources (Political Administration)

*Prithvipalanam: Retention of acquired resources
(Political Administration)*

Purushartha: Dharma, Artha, Kama and Moksha

Rajadharma: Duties towards the King (The code of laws)

Rajahrishi: The King or minister who is expertise in all these four sciences or Shastras. (HRD)

Rajaprakritis: Twelve Kingly constituents (The theory of Mandala)

Rajyadharma: Duties towards the state (The code of laws)

*Rajyadharmasthapana: The establishment of dharma or
righteousness in the royal throne (The code of laws)*

Rajyamandalathathwam: The Mandala or circle theory

Rajyasasana: The Commandments of the King (The code of laws)

Rakshasas: Giants

Rasadha: The secret Poisoners (Espionage)

Rashtram: Country side

Rathadhyakshan: Chief Commander of chariot corps

Roopikam: Manufacturing Charges (Economics)

Samahartr: Administrator

Samam: Conciliation (Conflict Management-HRD)

Samgrahanam: Administrative center or revenue Zone for a group of ten villages

Samsrayam: Seek support from others (Theory of Shadgunyam)

Samsthadhyakshan: Chief controller of private trading

*Samstham: A monitoring stationary squad to check the observation of four sciences/Shastras.
(Espionage)*

Sancharam: A monitoring mobile squad to check the observation of four sciences/Shastras. (Espionage)

Sandhi: Peace treaty (Theory of Shadgunyam)

Sarvadharmasthapana: Establish all righteousness (The code of laws)

Sasana: Royal edicts (The code of laws)

Sathrin: The secret agent in department of espionage

Seethadhyaksha: Chief Superintendent of crown lands/ Agriculture

Senabaktham: Army maintenance tax

Sethu: Irrigation Projects

Shadgunyathathwa: Six-fold theory

Smritis: Vedic text written by Manu.

Srenibalam: The people's power

Sthaneeyam: Administrative centre or districts for eight hundred villages

Sthanikan/Gopan: Taxes collected through Governor/ Record Keeper

Sthanikas: District Administrators

Sudra: The class that are privileged agriculture in Arthashastra

Sulkadhyaksha: Chief controller of custom and Octoroi

Sulkam: Customs Duty (Economics)

Sunadhyaksha: Chief conservator of animals and slaughter

Suradhyaksha: Chief controller of Alcoholic beverages

Suthradhyaksha: Chief textile commissioner

Suvarnadhyaksha: Chief Superintendent of precious metals

Swadharmasthapana: The establishment of Dharma or righteousness in the individual life of all classes

Swapakika: A type of tribe in Arthashastra

Thadhathwika: People who spoil their own wealth (Economics)

Thaksahsila: The well-known learning centre of ancient India

Thapasavyajna: Spies under the cover of ascetics (Espionage)

Theekshnas: The official in department of espionage

Thozhildharma: Duties towards job (The code of laws)

Thrayi: Three Vedas

Udhaseenam: The Neutral King (Theory of Mandala)

Udhasthitha: Spies under the cover of monks (Espionage)

*Upapradhanam: Placating with rewards and gifts
(Conflict Management-HRD)*

Uttishtatha! Jagrata! Prapya varannibhodhata!: -Arise, awake and stop not till the goal is reached
(The great saying of Vivekananda)

Vaidharanam: Counter veiling duties of tax (Economics)

Vaidhehars: The official in department of espionage

Vaishya: The class that are privileged for trade and commerce in Arthashastra

Vanam: Forests

Vanikpadam: Trade

Vartha: Three-fold economic theory comprised of agriculture, animal husbandry and trade and commerce in Arthashastra.

Varthani: Road cess (Economics)

Vigraham: Waging war (Theory of Shadgunyam)

Vijigishu: Conqueror (Theory of Mandala)

Vishti: Human resources or labour (HRD)

*Vivahasamyuktham: Law on marital relationships among the
17 code of laws in Arthashastra.*

Vividhadhyaksha: Chief controller of pasture lands

Vrajam: Animal Husbandry

Vyaji: Transaction Tax

Vyayapratyam: Savings from expenditure (Economics)

Vydhehakavyajna: Spies under the cover of merchants (Espionage)

Vyvahara: The witnesses (The code of laws)

Yanam: Prepare for war (Theory of Shadgunyam)

LIST OF FIGURES

26. The people and conflict management

27. Structure of Judiciary in Arthashastra

28. Kautilya code of laws.

29. The administration of countryside

30. The city administration in Arthashastra

31. Six-fold theory of political equilibrium

BIBLIOGRAPHY

1. Armstrong Michael, "Managing people, A Practical guide for Line Managers", Kogan Page, Crest Publishing House, New Delhi, 1999.

2. Backhouse, R.E., "Truth and Progress in Economic Knowledge", Cheltenham: Edward Elgar, 1997.

3. Balbir S. Sihag, "Accounting Historians Journal Dec 2004", Academy of Accounting Historians, University Of Massachusetts Lowell.

4. Bandopadhyaya Chandra Narayan. "Kautilya or an exposition of his social ideal and political theory", R. Canbray & Co., Culcutta, 1927.

5. Cushing, B. E., "A Kuhnian Interpretation of xth Historical Evolution of Accounting," Accounting Historians Journal, Vol. 16, No. 2: 1-41., 1989.

6. Datta K, Samar & Deodhar Y. Satish. "Implications of WTO agreements for Indian agriculture", Oxford & IBA Publishing Co.Pvt, Ltd, New Delhi, 2001.

7. Davis Miles, "Sri Chanakya Niti-Sastra;The Political Ethics Of Chanakya Pandit", Raja Ram Kumar Press, Lucknow, 1981.

8. Duening.N.Thomas, "Management Principles and guidelines", Himal Impressions, 168, Raja Garden, New Delhi, 2004.

9. Ezhuthachan K.N. "Bashakautaleeyam", Madras University, Madrass, 1960.

10. Godfrey-Smith, P., "Theory and Reality, an Introduction to the Philosophy of Science", Chicago: The University of Chicago Press, 2003.

11. Hahn, F. H., "Equilibrium and Macroeconomics", Oxford: Basil Blackwell, 1984.

12. Hall, R. E. and Jones, C. I., "The Productivity of Nations," National Bureau of Economic Research, Working Paper 5812, Cambridge: NBER, 1996.

13. Ifrah, G., "The Universal History of Numbers", New York: John Wiley & Sons, 2000.

14. Jolly, Julius.Dr. "Arthashastra of Kautilya", Vol-1, Motilal Banarsidas, 1923.

15. Jolly, Julius.Dr. "Arthashastra of Kautilya", Vol-2, Motilal Banarsidas, 1924.

16. K.V.M. "Kautilyante Arthashastram", Kerala Sahithya Academy, Thrissur, 1998.

17. Kangle, R. P. (1965), "The Kautilya Arthasastra", Part III (Delhi: Motilal Banarsidas), 2000 reprint.

18. Kangle, R.P. "The Kautilya Arthashastra", Part-1, II, III, Motilal Banarsidas, New Delhi, 2000.

19. Karl Marx & Engles Frederick." Manifesto of the Communist Party", English Edition, Progress Publishers, Moscow, 1977.

20. Kautilya, V. C. (4th Century B.C.E.), " The Kautilya Arthasastra", Part II, An English Translation with Critical and Explanatory Notes, 2nd Ed. 1972 by Kangle, R. P. (Delhi: Motilal Banarsidass), 2000 reprint.

21. Kautilya, V. C. (4th Century B.C.E.), "The Kautilya Arthasastra", Part I, Sanskrit Text with a Glossary, 2nd Ed. 1969 by Kangle, R. P. (Delhi: Motilal Banarsidass), 2000 reprint.

22. Kautilya, V.C, (4th Century B.C.E.), "The Arthashastra", Edited, Rearranged, Translated and Introduced by L. N. Rangarajan, New Delhi, New York: Penguin Books, 1992.

23. Keith, A.B. "A history of Sanskrit literature", Oxford, 1956.

24. Kossambi D.D. "Prachina Bharathathinte Samskaravum Nagarikathayum, Charithraparamaya Rooparekha", ICHRD, DC Books, Kottayam, 1981.

25. Lazear, E. P., "Economic Imperialism," Quarterly Journal of Economics, Vol. 115, No. 1: 99-146, 1999.

26. Lenin V. I., "State and Revolution", New York: International Publishers Co., Inc., 1932

27. Leonard Nadler, "Corporate Human Resource Development", Van Nostrand, New York, p.5, 1969.

28. Lipsey, R., Bekar, G. and Carlaw, K., "The Consequences of Changes in GPTs." In E. Helpman (ed.), General Purpose Technologies and Economic Growth, Cambridge, US: MIT Press, 193-218,1998b.

29. Lipsey, R., Bekar, G. and Carlaw, K., "What Requires Examination?" In E. Helpman (ed.), General Purpose Technologies and Economic Growth, Cambridge, US: MIT Press: 15-54, 1998a.

30. Mattessich, R., "Review and Extension of Bhattacharya's Modern Accounting Concepts in Kautilya's Arthasastra, Accounting, Business & Financial History", Vol. 8, No. 2: 191-209, 1998.

31. Mattessich, R., "The Beginnings of Accounting and Accounting History-Accounting Practice in the Middle East (8000 B. C. to 2000 B. C.) and Accounting Thought in India (300 B. C. and the Middle Ages) "New York: Garland Publishing, (2000).

32. Mital, S. N., "Kautilya Arthashastra Revisited", New Delhi: PHISPC, 2000.

33. Naik, B.B. "Ideals of ancient Hindu politics and Arthashastra of Kautilya", Karnataka printing works, Dharwar, 1932.

34. Nehru, J. (1946), "The Discovery of India", The Signet Press (New Delhi: Oxford University Press), 1998 reprint.

35. Parameswaran M. "Chanakyasutram", Aradhana Books, Thrissur.

36. Patrick Olivelle, "The Law code of Manu", Oxford University Press Inc., New York, 2004.

37. Post, J. E., Lawrence, A. T. and Weber, J., "Business and Society", 10th ed. Boston: McGraw-Hill, 2002.

38. Rangarajan, L.N. "The Kautilya Arthashastra", Penguin Books, New Delhi, 1992.

39. Ray, B. N., "Tradition and Innovation in Indian Political Thought", Delhi: Ajanta Books International, 1999.

40. Sahithya Pravarthaka Sangham. "Sarwavijnanakosa", Book 1&5, NBS, Kottayam, 1981

41. Sensarma, P. "Ethnobilological information in Kautilya Arthashastra", Durbar offset Pvt. Ltd., Culcutta, 1998.

42. Shama Sastry, R. "Arthashastra of Kautilya", Govt. Branch Press, Mysore, 1924.

43. Shamashastry R.Dr. "Kautilya's Arthashastra", The Indian Antiquary, A Journal Of Oriental Research, Vol. XXXIV, 1905

44. Spengler, J. J., "Indian Economic Thought", Durham: Duke University Press, 1971.

45. Spiegel, H. W., "The Growth of Economic Thought", 3rd Ed., Durham: Duke University Press, 1991.

46. Stigler, G. J., "Economics - The Imperial Science," Scandinavian Journal of Economics, Vol. 86, No. 3: 301-313, 1984.

47. Subha Rao, P.Dr. "Essentials of Human Resource Management and Industrial relations", Himalaya Publishing house, 1996.

48. Subramanian, V. K. (1980), "Maxims of Chanakya" (New Delhi: Shakti Malik, Abhinav Publications), 2000 reprint.

49. Sukumar Azhikode. " Bharatheeyatha", D.C. Books, Kottayam, 1995.

50. Swami Vivekananda. "Caste, Culture and Socialism", Express Printers, Pvt. Ltd, Culcutta, 1975.

51. Vekateswara Rao.T., "Integrated Human Resource Development Systems" in T.V.Rao and D.F. Pereira, " Recent Experiences in HRD, Oxford & IBH Publishing Co.Ltd., New Delhi, 1986, pp.3-4.

52. VirendraKumar M.P, Vasudevan P.A. "Lokavyapara sanghatanayum oorakudukukalum", Mathrubhumi, Kozhikode, 2002.

53. Visakadhathan. "Mudhrarakshasam", Translation, Kalpetta Balakrishnan, Current Books, Thrissur, 1989.

54. Weber Albrecht, "The history of Indian literature", Kegan Paul, Trench Trubner & Co. Ltd, London, 1914.

www.ingramcontent.com/pod-product-compliance
Lightning Source LLC
Chambersburg PA
CBHW022006170526
45157CB00003B/1173